evita by evita

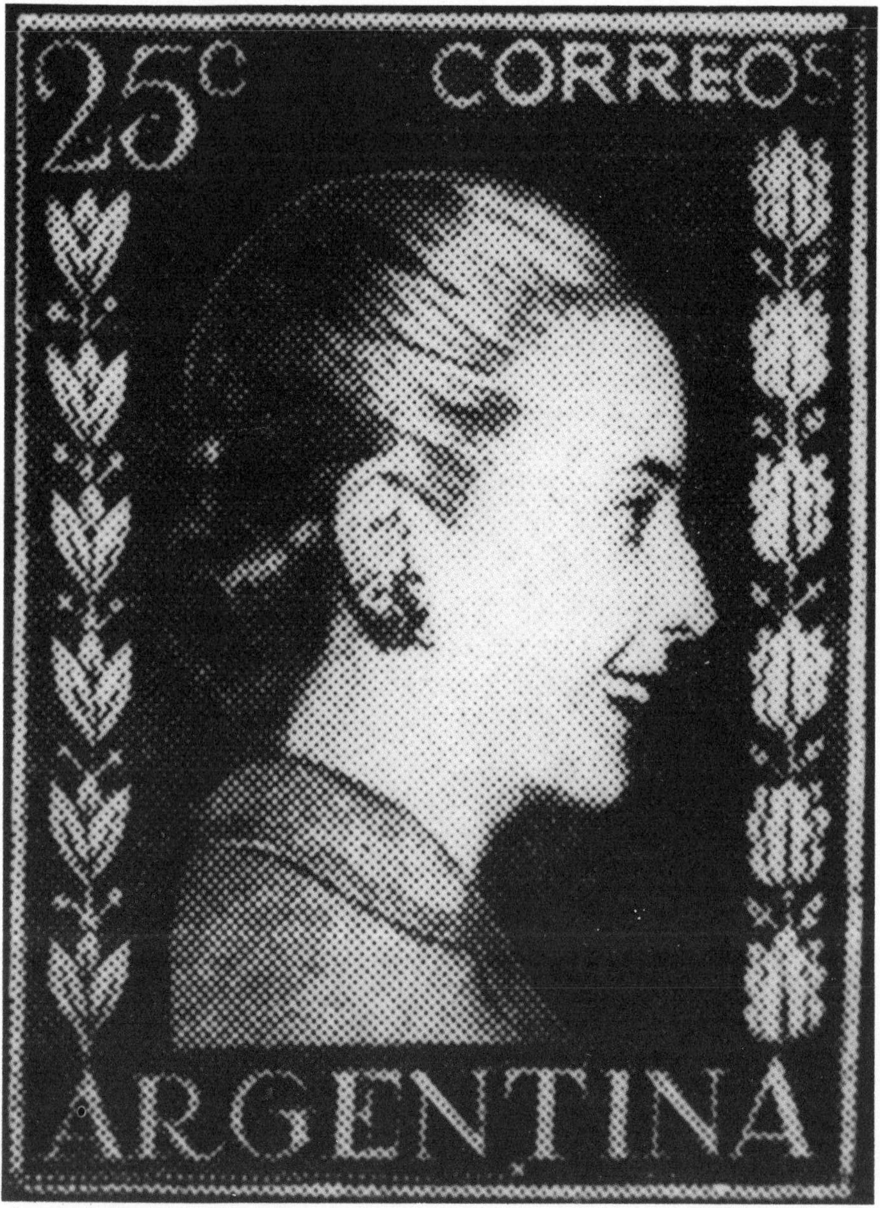
25c
CORREOS
ARGENTINA

evita by evita

Eva Duarte Perón Tells Her Own Story

PROTEUS

PROTEUS BOOKS is an imprint of
The Proteus Publishing Group

United Kingdom
PROTEUS (PUBLISHING) LIMITED
Bremar House,
Sale Place,
London, W2 1PT

United States
PROTEUS PUBLISHING CO., INC.
distributed by:
THE SCRIBNER BOOK COMPANIES, INC.
597 Fifth Avenue
New York, N.Y. 10017

ISBN 0 906071 05 4

First published as *La Razon De Mi Vida* 1953
This edition with appendices first published June 1978
Paperback edition first published May 1980
Second Printing, November 1980
© 1953 Juan Domingo Peron
All rights reserved

Printed and bound in U.S.
by THE BOOK PRESS

Contents

Prologue

This book has sprung from my innermost heart. However much I speak in its pages of my feelings, of my thoughts and of my life, in all that I have written the least observant of my readers will find nothing else but the figure, the soul and the life of General Perón and my profound love for him and for his cause.

Many will reproach me for thinking only of him while having written all this; I confess in advance that it is true, absolutely true.

And I have my reasons, my powerful reasons, which nobody will be able to dispute or doubt: I was not, nor am I, anything more than a humble woman . . . a sparrow in an immense flock of sparrows. . . . But Perón was, and is, a gigantic condor that flies high and sure among the summits and near to God. If it had not been for him who came down to my level and taught me to fly in another fashion, I would never have known what a condor is like, nor ever have been able to contemplate the marvelous and magnificent immenseness of my people.

That is why neither my life nor my heart belongs to me, and nothing of all that I am or have is mine. All that I am, all that I have, all that I think and all that I feel, belongs to Perón.

But I do not forget, nor will I ever forget, that I was a sparrow, nor that I am still one. If I fly higher, it is through him. If I walk among the peaks, it is through him. If sometimes I almost touch the sky with my wings, it is through him. If I see clearly what my people are, and love them and feel their affection caressing my name, it is solely through him.

That is why I dedicate to him, wholly, this song which, like that of the sparrow, has no beauty, but is humble and sincere, and contains all the love of my heart.

EVA PERON *1952*

PART ONE
The Causes of My Mission

1

A Case of Chance?

MANY PERSONS CANNOT understand the circumstances which have made my life what it is.

I myself have often pondered on all this that is now my life.

Some of my contemporaries attribute it all to chance—that strange and inexplicable thing that does not explain anything, anyway.

No. It is not chance that has brought me to this position, to this life I lead.

Obviously it would all be absurd if my sharpest-tongued critics were right when they say thoughtlessly that I, "a superficial woman, uninstructed, common, unacquainted with the interests of her country, remote from the sorrows of her people, indifferent to social justice and with nothing serious in her head, suddenly became a fanatic in the struggle for the cause of the people, and, making that cause hers, decided to live a life of incomprehensible sacrifice."

I would like to make myself clear about this.

That is why I have decided to write these notes.

But I do not do so to contradict anyone or to prove anyone wrong.

Rather I would wish my fellow citizens, men and women, to know how I feel and think.

3

I want them to share in the great things I experience in my heart.

Surely many of the things I shall say here are teachings I received freely from Perón and which I have not the right to keep secret.

2

A Great Feeling

I HAVE TO look back on the course of my life to find the earliest reason for all that is happening to me now.

Perhaps I am wrong in saying "the earliest *reason*," since the truth is that all my life I have been prone to be driven and guided by my feelings.

Even today, in this rush of things that I must perform, I let myself be guided very often—in fact almost always—primarily by what I feel.

Reason, with me, often has to give way to emotion; and so, to explain the life I lead today, that is to say, what I am doing now out of motives that spring from the bottom of my heart, I have to go back and search through my earliest years for the first feelings that make sense, or at least explain, what to those severe critics is "an incomprehensible sacrifice," but which to me is neither sacrifice nor incomprehensible.

I have discovered a fundamental feeling in my heart which completely governs my spirit and my life. That feeling is my *indignation when confronted with injustice.*

Ever since I can remember, all injustice has hurt my soul as though something were stabbing it. Memories of injustices against which I rebelled at every age still rankle.

I remember very well how sad I was for many days when I

first realized that there were poor and rich in the world; and the strange thing is that the fact of the existence of the poor did not hurt me so much as the knowledge that, at the same time, the rich existed.

3
The Cause of the "Incomprehensible Sacrifice"

THE SUBJECT OF the rich and the poor has been, ever since, the subject of my musings. I think I never mentioned it to other people, not even to my mother, but I thought about it often.

I still needed, however, to take a step forward along the path of my discoveries.

I knew that there were poor and that there were rich; and I knew that the poor were more numerous than the rich, and were to be found everywhere.

I had yet to learn the third dimension of injustice.

Until I was eleven years old I believed that there were poor just as there was grass, and that there were rich just as there were trees.

One day I heard for the first time, from the lips of a working-man, that there were poor because the rich were too rich; and that revelation made a strong impression on me.

I connected that opinion with all the things I had thought of on the subject . . . and, almost instantaneously, I realized that the man was right. Even more than through the power of reason, I felt that it was true.

Furthermore, although so young, I had already come to

believe more in what the poor said than in the words of the rich, because the former seemed to me more sincere, franker, and also better. With this step I had come to know the third dimension of social injustice.

This third step in the discovery of life and its social problems is, indubitably, taken by many people. The majority of men and women know that there are poor because there are rich, but they learn it unconsciously, and perhaps because of that it seems natural and logical to them.

I admit I learned it almost at one blow, and that I learned it through suffering; and I declare that it never seemed to me either logical or natural.

I felt, even then, in my innermost heart, something which I now recognize as a feeling of indignation. I did not understand why if there were poor people there must also be rich ones, nor why the latter's eagerness for riches must be the cause of the poverty of so many people.

Never since then have I been able to think of this injustice without indignation, and thinking about it always produced a stifling feeling, as though, being unable to remedy the evil that I witnessed, I had not sufficient air to breathe.

I think now that many people become accustomed to social injustice in the first years of their lives. Even the poor think the misery they endure is natural and logical. They learn to tolerate what they see or suffer, just as it is possible to acquire a tolerance for a powerful poison.

I cannot accustom myself to poison, and never, since I was eleven years old, have I been able to accustom myself to social injustice.

This is, perhaps, the only inexplicable thing of my life; certainly it is the only thing which manifested itself in me without any apparent cause.

I think that, just as some persons have a special tendency to feel beauty differently and more intensely than do people in general, and therefore become poets or painters or musicians, I have a special inherent tendency to feel injustice with unusual and painful intensity.

Can a painter say why he sees and feels color? Can a poet explain why he is a poet?

Perhaps that is why I can never say *why* I feel pained by injustice, and why I have never been able to accept it as a natural thing, as the majority of men accept it.

Still, even if I cannot understand it myself, it is certain that my feeling of indignation at social injustice is the force which has led me by the hand, since my earliest recollections, to this day . . . and that it is the final cause explaining how a woman who in some people's eyes sometimes seems "superficial, common and indifferent," can decide to live a life of "incomprehensible sacrifice."

4

Someday All Will Change

I NEVER THOUGHT, however, that it would fall to my lot to take such a direct part in my countrymen's fight for social justice.

I, a weak woman, after all, never imagined that the serious problem of the poor and the rich would one day knock so directly at the door of my heart, claiming my humble efforts for its solution in my country.

As I grew older, so too did the problem encompass me more each day. Perhaps, because of that, I tried to run away from myself, to forget my one obsession; and I dedicated myself intently to my unusually strong artistic vocation.

I recollect that, as a child, I always wanted to recite. It was as though I always wished to tell others something—something great which I felt, deep in my heart.

Now, whenever I speak to my fellow citizens, I feel I am expressing that "something" which I tried to say when I recited at my school festivals!

My artistic vocation acquainted me with other scenes. I left off noticing common, everyday injustices, and began to glimpse at first, and learn afterward of, great injustices; and I found them not only in the fiction I portrayed but also in the realities of my new life.

I did not want to see, to understand, to look at misfortune, grief and misery; but the more I wished to forget about injustice, the more I was surrounded by it.

Signs of social injustice in the life of our country appeared to me at every step, at every turn of the way, and hedged me in on every side every day.

Little by little, my deep feeling of indignation against injustice overflowed the cup of my soul, reaching the limit of silence, and I began to take part in a few struggles.

They had nothing to do with me personally, and I gained nothing by interfering; all I achieved was to get on the wrong side of those who, to my manner of thinking, unmercifully exploited other people's weakness. It was gradually getting too much for my powers, and my best intentions to "shut up" and "not interfere" fell to the ground at the first provocation.

In this way my inner rebelliousness began to manifest itself.

I realize that sometimes my response was unwarranted and my words and actions exaggerated in proportion to the injury which had provoked me.

But I was retaliating against more than that specific injustice—rather, against all injustice.

It was my form of relief, my liberation; and relief, like freedom, often tends to be exaggerated, above all when the oppressing force is very great.

Sometimes, in one of these retaliations of mine, I remember saying: "Someday all this will change" . . . and I do not know whether this was a prayer or a curse, or both.

Although the phrase is common to all revolt, I comforted myself with it as though I believed firmly in what I was saying. Perhaps I already believed then that someday everything would be different, but naturally I did not know how or when—and still less did I guess that fate would give me a place, a very humble one, but after all a place, in the task of liberation.

There were many more poor than rich in the spot where I spent my childhood, but I tried to convince myself that there must be other places in my country and in the world where things happened otherwise.

I imagined, for instance, that great cities were wonderful

places where there were only riches; and all I heard said confirmed this belief of mine. The great city was spoken of as a marvelous paradise where everything was lovely and unusual, and I almost imagined, from what was said, that even the people there were more worthy than those in my town.

One day—I must have been seven years old—I visited the city for the first time. When I got there I found that it was not what I had imagined. On arrival I saw its poverty-stricken districts, and by the varying appearance of the streets and houses I knew that there were poor and rich in the city also.

That evidence must have hurt me deeply, for today, every time I return to the city from my travels in the interior of the country, I recall that first contact with its grandeur and its misery, and feel again the sensation of inner sadness I then experienced.

Only once in my life have I felt similarly disillusioned; it was when I learned that the Three Wise Men did not really come on camels with their gifts.

Thus my discovery that there were poor in the city also, and therefore that they must be everywhere, all over the world, left a painful impression on my heart.

That very day I discovered that the poor were indubitably more numerous than the rich, and not only among my people but everywhere.

5

I Resign Myself as a Victim

ONE DAY I glanced, through natural curiosity, at the press which claimed to belong to the people.

I looked for company. Isn't it true that almost always, in the books and newspapers we read, we look more for company than for a path to follow or a guide to lead us?

Perhaps that is why I read our country's leftist press. But I did not find there either company, or a path, and still less anything to guide me.

The "papers of the people" condemned, it is true, in hard and strong language, capitalism, and also certain of the wealthy, pointing out the defects of the loathsome social regime which our country suffered.

But in the details, and even at the core of their doctrine, it was easy to discern the influence of distant ideas, very remote from everything Argentine: foreign systems and formulas strange to our land and our feelings.

It could clearly be seen that what they wanted for the Argentine people did not come from the people themselves. And this corroboration put me immediately on my guard.

Another thing also disgusted me. Their formula for the solution of social injustice was a common system—the same for all countries and for all peoples. I could not believe that, even to

15

destroy so great an evil, it should be necessary to attack and annihilate anything as natural and as great as the nation.

Here I want to explain that in this country, until recent years, many (salaried) trade-union leaders considered that the nation and its symbols were, like religion, prejudiced in favour of capitalism.

Their changeover afterward is another reason why I distrust the sincerity of these "ardent defenders of the people."

Reading the leftist newspapers led me, it is true, to the conclusion that social injustice in my country could be wiped out only by a revolution; but I could not accept the idea that this must be an international revolution, coming from without and created by men foreign to our ways and thoughts.

I could understand only domestic remedies, solving obvious problems; simple solutions, not complicated economic theories; in a word, patriotic solutions, as national as the very people they were meant to save.

"Why increase further," I asked myself, "the misfortune of those suffering from injustice, by taking the vision of the nation and of faith out of the world they are accustomed to contemplate?"

I thought it would be like taking the sky out of a landscape.

Why, instead of constantly attacking the country, and religion, did not the "leaders of the people" try to put these moral forces at the service of the salvation of the people?

I suspected that those persons strove more to weaken the nation and its moral forces than to secure the well-being of the workers.

I did not like this remedy for the evil.

I knew little, but my heart and common sense guided me; and I returned to my former thoughts, my own thoughts, convinced I had nothing to do with that kind of struggle.

The indignation that rose in my heart at the solutions they proposed, and at the disloyalty of the presumed "leaders of the people," was added to my natural indignation at social injustice.

I resigned myself to be a victim.

6

My Marvelous Day

IN EVERY LIFE there comes what seems a definite moment.

It is the day one thinks one has started on a smooth, monotonous path, with no turnings, without any new outlooks. And one believes that life will always be made up of the same things, the same daily tasks—that its course is definitely set.

That, more or less, is what happened to me at that moment of my life.

I said I had resigned myself to be a victim. Further, I had resigned myself to leading an ordinary, monotonous life. Such a life, I thought, would be fruitless, but that I must lead it seemed inevitable. And I saw no way of getting away from it. Also, that life of mine, troubled in spite of its monotony, left me no time for anything.

But at the bottom of my soul I could not resign myself to the fact that it should be forever.

At last "my marvelous day" came.

All of us, or nearly all, have a marvelous day in our lives.

For me it was the day my life coincided with the life of Perón.

The meeting left an indelible mark on my heart; and I cannot omit a description of it, because it meant the beginning of my real life.

17

I know now that men are classified into two groups. One, infinitely numerous, is composed of those engaged in ordinary, everyday activities; who move only along known paths already explored by others. They content themselves with achieving success. The other group, small—very small—is made up of men who place extraordinary value on all they have to do. These are not content except with glory. They breathe the air of the coming century, which will sing their glories; they live almost in eternity.

To them, a new path always holds an irresistible attraction. For Alexander, it was the road to Persia; for Columbus, a western route to the Indies; for Napoleon, the way which he thought led to world empire; for José de San Martin, the path which brought liberty to South America.

The man I met belonged to this class of men.

What he was about to accomplish in my country was nothing less than a revolution.

When the thing to be accomplished is a revolution, the group of men capable of following its course to the end sometimes diminishes to the vanishing point.

Many revolutions have been started here and in every country of the world. But a revolution always entails a new path whose course is difficult, and which is meant only for those who feel the irresistible attraction of dangerous enterprises.

That is why revolutions wished for by the people, and even carried out with their entire support, have failed, and continue to fail.

When the Second World War somewhat loosened the influence of the imperialists protecting the oligarchy enthroned in the government of our country, a group of men decided to bring about the revolution that the people wanted.

And so that group of men set out on the new road; but after the first encounters with its hard realities and difficulties, the majority of the revolutionists began to follow the same course as in other revolutions . . . and the revolution was left in mid-air, half completed, remaining in the hopes of the people as something still to be accomplished.

Nevertheless, one man insisted on advancing along the difficult path.

From the watchtower of my old inner restlessness I saw him appear. He was obviously different from the rest. Others cried "Fire!" and ordered the advance.

He cried "Fire!" and himself advanced, decided and tenacious, in one direction only, not halted by any obstacle.

At that moment I felt that his cry and his path were my own cry and my own path.

I put myself at his side. Perhaps that attracted his attention, and when he could listen to me I ventured to tell him, in my best language: "If it is as you say, the cause of the people is my own cause; however great the sacrifice, I will not leave your side until I faint."

He accepted my offer.

That was "my marvelous day."

7

Yes, This is the Man of my People!

SOON, FROM THE wayside, the "ordinary man" began to throw stones at us: threats, insults and slanders.

The "ordinary men" are the eternal enemies of anything new, of all progress, of every out-of-the-ordinary idea—and, therefore, of all revolution.

That is why someone has said that the mediocre man is the fiercest and most rigid enemy of the man of genius.

Everything out of the ordinary is to them unpardonable madness, exaggerated and dangerous fanaticism.

I have seen them, and I still see them, looking at me with "compassion" and "mercy"—with that air of superiority that characterizes them.

They will never understand how and why anyone can do anything different from the things they themselves think of, and they never do anything that is not for themselves!

They saw Perón come forward. First they laughed at him, believing and even saying that he was mad.

But when they discovered that the madman had kindled a fire, and that the conflagration was spreading on all sides and already touching their interests and ambitions, then they became frightened and, going underground, swore that he should disappear.

They did not count on the people. It had never occurred to them to think of the people, or to imagine that the people themselves could sometimes carry out their own will and decide their own destiny.

Why didn't the humble men, the workers of my country, take the same attitude as the "ordinary men," instead of understanding Perón and believing in him?

There is only one explanation: that one needs only to see Perón to believe in him, in his sincerity, in his loyalty and in his openness.

They saw him, and believed.

What happened in Bethlehem nearly two thousand years ago was repeated here. The first to believe were not the rich, not the wise, not the powerful, but the humble.

For almost always the rich, the wise and the powerful are hedged in by egoism and selfishness.

On the other hand, the poor, as at Bethlehem, live and sleep in the open air, and the windows of their simple souls are almost always open to out-of-the-ordinary things.

That is why they saw and believed. They also saw that a man was risking all for them. I know well how many times he risked all for his people on one single throw.

Happily, he won. Otherwise he would have lost everything, including his life.

I, meanwhile, kept my promise to "be at his side."

I held the lamp that lighted his darkness; I kept it burning as best I knew how, guarding his flank with my love and with my faith.

Often I saw him from a corner in his office in the loved Secretariat of Labor and Welfare, listening to the humble workingmen of my country, speaking to them of their problems, giving them the explanations they had been craving for many years. Never will those first pictures of our life together be erased from my memory.

There I knew him frank and cordial, sincere and humble, generous and untiring; there I glimpsed the greatness of his soul and the fearlessness of his heart.

Seeing him, my spirit broadened as if all this were sky and pure air. The old anguish of my heart began to melt within me like frost and snow under the sun. And I felt infinitely happy. And I said to myself, with ever increasing emphasis: "Yes, this is the man. This is the man of my people. No one can compare with him."

And when I saw him clasp the hard and horny hands of the workers I could not help thinking that in him and by him my people, for the first time, were shaking hands with happiness.

8

My Hour of Loneliness

THE CONFLAGRATION CONTINUED to advance with us.

The "ordinary men" of the comfortable and easy-going oligarchy began to think that the firebrand must be disposed of. They thought that would put out the flames.

At last they decided to carry out their plans.

This happened in Argentina's last hours of oligarchy. Afterwards, the dawn . . .!

For nearly eight days they had Perón in their hands.

I was not in prison with him, but in recollection those eight days still hurt me—and more, far more, than if I had been able to spend them in his company, sharing his anguish.

From the start he advised me to be calm. I must say I never saw him so magnificent in his serenity. I remember that a friendly ambassador came to offer him the sanctuary of a foreign nation. With a few words and a simple gesture he decided to stay in his own country, to face it out among his own.

From the time that Perón went until the people recovered him for itself—and for me!—my days were filled with pain and fever.

I rushed into the streets looking for friends who might still be able to do something for him.

Thus I went from door to door. In that painful and incessant walking I felt the flame of his fire burning in my heart, consuming my utter smallness.

I wandered about all the districts of the great city. Ever since then I have known all the kinds of hearts that beat under my country's sky.

As I went down from the proud and rich districts to the poor and the humble, doors began to open more generously, with more cordiality.

Above, I had found only cold, calculating hearts, "prudent" hearts of "ordinary men " incapable of thinking or of doing anything out of the ordinary; hearts whose contact brought me nausea, disgust and shame.

This was the worst of my Calvary about the great city. The cowardice of the men who could have done something and did not, washing their hands like Pilate, hurt me more than the rude fisticuffs given me when a group of cowards denounced me, yelling: "That is Evita!'

These blows, on the other hand, did me good.

At every blow I thought I would die, and yet at every blow I felt reborn. Something rough, but at the same time ineffable, was that baptism of pain which purified me of all doubt and of all cowardice.

Had I not said to him, 'However great the sacrifice, I will not leave your side until I faint"?

Since that day I think it cannot be very difficult to die for a cause that one loves. Or, simply, to die for love.

9

A Great Light

I CHERISH MANY memories of those days of anguish and bitterness.

Alongside the shadows formed by the treachery and cowardice of many, there appear, among my memories, gestures lit with loyalty and valor.

But I do not yet want to write in detail about all that.

That week in October, 1945, was a panorama of many shadows and of many lights. It were better not to get too close to it . . . and to look at it another time, from farther off. This does not prevent me from saying, however, with absolute frankness, in anticipation of what I will write in detail some day, that the light came only from the people.

In this book, which tries to set forth the causes and the objects of the mission to which I have dedicated myself, I cannot omit the following episode. It figures in my spirit as a fundamental reason for what I am at this hour of my country's history, and it led me to the post I now occupy in the justicialist[1] movement.

I recall that in my loneliness and bitterness, while I wandered about the great city, I expected at every instant to receive some message from the absent and imprisoned Leader. I

[1]From *Justicialismo*, General Perón's political doctrine.

imagined that in some way he would contrive to let me know how he was and where he was; and I awaited his news with a soul tortured by anguish.

I keep the various messages he wrote me in those days; and in all of them the calmness of spirit with which he faced events is evidenced by his clear, firm and decisive handwriting.

In these messages he repeatedly asked me to recommend his workers to be calm, not to worry about him, not to create violent incidents.

I—I confess it honestly—searched in all his letters for a word that would tell me of his love.

Instead, he hardly spoke of anything but his "workers" . . . whom at that time the oligarchy, at large in the streets, began to call *descamisados*.[1]

His strange insistence enlightened me. "To you I entrust my workers" were his words of love, his most heartfelt words of love.

This revelation brought—and still does—a great light into my life. To me, a humble and lowly woman, he entrusted the care of his workers, his greatest love. And I thought to myself: "He could have entrusted them to others, to any of his friends, including some trade-union leader . . . but no, he wanted it to be me . . . a woman who knows nothing except how to love him!'

That was, without a doubt, proof positive of his love. But it was a proof that required an answer; and I gave it to him.

I gave it to him then, and I keep on giving it. As long as I live I will not forget that he, Perón, entrusted me with his *descamisados* in the most difficult hour of his life.

As long as I live I will not forget that he, when he wished to prove his love to me, trusted me to look after his workers!

He found no better way of expressing his love, and I am sure now that he chose the purest and greatest way of telling me of it.

Ever since that day, whenever I, in turn, want to show him my womanly love—and I always want to show it—I cannot find

[1]"Shirtless ones," a designation equivalent to the *sans-culottes* of the French Revolution.

either a purer or a greater way than of offering him a little of my life, burning it up with love for his *descamisados*.

This, also, is part of my debt of gratitude to him and to them, and I discharge it gladly, happily, as one fulfills all the debts imposed by love.

10

Vocation and Destiny

NO. CHANCE WAS not the cause of all that I now mean to my country and to my people. I firmly believe that I was shaped for the work I perform and the life I lead.

When I analyze, in my soul, the reason for my existence, I am more and more convinced that luck and chance are lies.

If luck and chance governed the world, all would be chaos; and we could not live in such a grotesque scene. No luck does not govern the destiny of the world, nor yet of men. Fortunately, thank God, things happen in another way—in another way which some call Destiny and some call Providence, and which nearly all of us attribute to God.

I believe firmly that there really exists an unknown force which prepares men and women for the accomplishment of the particular mission which each of them must perform.

Whether this force is marvelously divine, or has been put by God into the nature of society or the human soul, I do not know, nor do I try to ascertain. But I believe it exists, and that it leads us without compulsion as long as we do not deny it our help.

What is certain is that this spiritual explanation is also more productive than the one which holds that blind chance rules. He who thinks he is the child of fortune does not feel compelled

31

to do anything, since luck is impersonal and can make no demands of any kind; but he who knows himself to be a child of Destiny or Providence, or of a force unknown but of an origin superior to his life and to his nature, must feel himself responsible for the mission entrusted him.

Forgive me these explanations. Without my wishing it, they have almost gone to the length of introducing a certain philosophical note, which I did not intend should be the case.

Nevertheless, I think it proper to have said all that I have, in the first place because I feel it that way, and in the second because it seems to me a matter of simple common sense.

My life is proof of all that I have said. If I had not become what I am, my entire life would remain unexplained.

Why have I always suffered in the face of injustice?

Why did I never resign myself to view the existence of poor and rich as natural and logical? Why did I always feel indignant in the presence of the possessors of power and wealth who exploited the humble and poor?

Why could I never free myself from that inner, stifling anguish?

Why, until "my marvelous day," did I feel lonely, disturbed, as though my life had no meaning, no reason?

Too many questions would have remained unanswered if I had not found Perón on my journey and, in him, discovered the cause of my people.

No. It is not chance that puts men and women at the head of great causes.

On the contrary, it seems as though great causes prepare the souls of the men and women who are to lead them. This may be, in part, vocation, but there is evidently something else which we cannot explain and which is not subject to the luck of chance.

That is why I must be allowed to continue insisting on this subject in a few more words, which I wish to be of humble counsel.

I think that if anyone finds himself suddenly carried to a post of responsibility in the fight for a great cause, he should search in his life and in his past for some explanation, and he will be sure to find it.

In this way he will realize all the weight of his responsibility, and work the more loyally for the cause he serves.

And I also think that those who happen to be spectators of such an event should not attribute it, without further thought, to chance. Would it not be more sensible to acknowledge the presence of something more?

And, mark, I do not say that it is directly God who determines all these things, but certainly that, in His magnificent ordering of all laws and of all forces, He must have created some law or force that leads those who freely and generously allow themselves to be guided.

This is the humble explanation I give of my life and of my position.

Among Perón's manuscripts I keep one he wrote on a similar theme shortly after assuming the presidency.

In this rough draft he touched with his habitual frankness on this strange matter of vocation and destiny.

It seems to me better to repeat it just as he wrote it, and, as all his soul appears in it in its simplicity and greatness—let us say in its essence—I save myself the weighty responsibility of explaining it . . . a thing, I confess, that would be beyond my power.

To know what the sun is like, a description or a painting is not sufficient; and no one, unless he is mad, tries to paint or describe it. To know what it is like, one has to go out and look at it, and, even looking at it, one cannot see it without being dazzled.

Here are his words and his thoughts, his soul and his heart. I limit myself to suggesting that we go out and see him.

11

On My Election[1]

IN THE LIVES of peoples, as in the lives of men, everything is not done by destiny.

It is necessary for peoples, like men, to help their destiny.

In my life, as in the life of my people, this was literally accomplished.

I am at the head of my people not only by a decree of destiny. I am there because, without knowing it perhaps, I prepared myself for it as though I had known that someday this responsibility and privilege would be my lot.

I can affirm and demonstrate also that my people, too, prepared patiently, although unwittingly, for this hour of its destiny.

What Providence does is to arrange the necessary circumstances so that things happen subsequently in one way and not another. But things almost always happen through our "fault."

Often I think that had I been born in any other part of my country perhaps I should not be today President of the Republic.

Because had I been born elsewhere, my surroundings would have given me other inclinations . . . I would not have chosen a military career, would not have learned there the things I did learn, would never have found myself obliged to start a revolution . . . These things are in the hands of Providence!

[1]From the memoirs of General Perón.

Providence combines infinite circumstances, and I do not believe that one can discover why, or explain anything of its mechanism.

All the rest we do ourselves!

Thus it was that one day I found myself in circumstances which decided my destiny.

The country was alone. It was off its course, unguided and without a compass. All had been handed to foreigners. The people, lacking justice, were oppressed and incapable. Foreign countries and international forces submitted them to a dominion not far removed from colonial oppression.

I realized that it could all be remedied.

Little by little it dawned on me that it was I who could remedy it.

From that moment my country's problem came to be my own problem.

I solved it by deciding on the revolution.

This decision was "my aid to Destiny."

Two and a half years later everything appeared to be lost.

I had striven intensely in the Secretariat of Labor and Welfare.

The people had understood me. My country's workers already knew the meaning of social justice and followed me almost as though I were a banner.

All I had done was to tell them the truth and give them what everyone up to then had denied them.

But the conspiring forces of the oligarchy and of international powers were stronger at one period than the people and my will.

It was in October of 1945.

All that is history.

For eight days I experienced all the shades of loneliness, desertion and bitterness.

Just as I had been thinking one day that it was necessary to start a revolution, the people felt—the people feel!—that a crucial moment in its history had come.

It realized that all was lost but that all might be saved.

Luckily it realized that this would depend on its decision.

And it decided.

All the rest was done by Providence . . . but the decision was taken by the people . . . its decision was "the help lent by the people to Destiny."

Those are the reasons for my election.

Two decisions at two providential moments.

But to provide a decision at a providential moment one has to be prepared for it beforehand.

I was prepared by life itself: my parents' home, my childhood in wild Patagonia, my military career, my life in the mountains, my journeys to Europe . . . all these had accustomed me to conquer. To conquer Nature is more difficult than to lead and control men, and it had often fallen to my lot to struggle with the forces of Nature and overcome them.

All this had prepared me to be able to feel deeply the lot of my people.

This prepared me for the moment of decision.

For the people, in its turn, to take the decision to save me in October, 1945, and then entrust me with the guidance of its destiny, it was also necessary to carry out a task of preparation.

This consisted of something like an awakening.

From 1943 to 1945 the people were awaking from an old lethargy which had lasted more than a century. But during that century they had lived on their ancient glories. The exploits of their grenadiers could not be forgotten by half a continent. Their thirst for liberty and justice could not be forgotten. That is why it was easy for me to awaken them. It was sufficient for me to dwell upon the old themes of the initial hours of their life: justice, liberty, independence and sovereignty.

Evidently my election is not a thing of chance. Providence played its part without a doubt, and for that I always thank God.

But the people and I helped.

The key to the future dwells precisely in taking care that this does not cease happening among us.

12

"Too Peronista"

ANYONE WHO HAS read the preceding chapter can readily understand that it is Perón's greatness, mixed with the simplicity of his genial nature, which makes me what I am, fervently and fanatically "Peronista."

Sometimes the Leader himself is wont to tell me fondly that I am "too Peronista."

I remember one afternoon when, after I had been talking to him for a long time of . . . of what would I be speaking to him except of himself, of his dreams, of his achievements, of his doctrine, of his triumphs? . . . he interrupted me to say: "You talk to me so much about Perón that I shall end by hating him." So anyone who searches in these pages for my portrait should not be surprised instead to find the figure of Perón.

It is—I admit it—that I have stopped being myself and it is he who exists in my soul, owner of all my speech and my feelings, absolute owner of my heart and of my life.

On the other hand, this is an old miracle, an ancient miracle of love, which by dint of repetition in the world no longer seems to us a miracle.

One day I was told that I was too Peronista to head a movement by the women of my country. I thought it over a good deal, and although I felt immediately that it was not true, I tried for

39

some time to learn why it was neither logical nor reasonable.

Yes, I am Peronista, fanatically Peronista.

Not too much. It would be too much if Peronism were not, as it is, the cause of a man who, by identifying himself with the cause of an entire people, is himself of infinite worth. And when confronted by infinite things, it is impossible to praise them too highly.

Perón says I am "too Peronista" because he cannot measure his own greatness by the yardstick of his humility.

Others—those who think, without telling me so, that I am too Peronista—come under the category of the "ordinary man." And these do not deserve an answer.

Because I am a Peronista, I cannot lead a woman's movement in my country? That indeed deserves an explanation!

"How," they asked me, "are you going to direct a woman's movement if you are fanatically in love with the cause of a man? Is not that a total acknowledgement of the superiority of man over woman? Isn't that a contradiction?"

No. It isn't. I felt it. Now I know it.

The truth, logical and reasonable, is that feminism cannot be separated from the very nature of woman.

And it is natural for woman to give herself, to surrender herself, for love; for in that surrender is her glory, her salvation, her eternity.

Then may not the best woman's movement in the world be, perhaps, that which gives itself for love of the cause and of the doctrine of a man who has proved to be one in every sense of the word?

In the same manner that a woman attains eternity and her glory, and saves herself from loneliness and from death by giving herself for love of a man, I think that perhaps no woman's movement will be glorious and lasting in the world if it does not give itself to the cause of a man.

What is important is that the cause and the man be worthy of such a total surrender.

I believe that Perón and his cause are sufficiently great and worthy to receive the total offering of the woman's movement of

40

my country. And, further, all the women of the world may support his justicialism; for with it, surrendering themselves for love of a cause which is that of humanity, they will increase in womanliness.

And if it is true that the cause itself will grow in glory by receiving them, it is not less true that they will be exalted by the surrender.

That is why I am and shall be Peronista until my dying day: because Perón's cause exalts me, and because its productiveness will continue forever in the works I perform for him, and live in posterity after I am gone.

But not only am I Peronista because of Perón's cause. I am a Peronista because of him personally, and I would not be able to say which of the two reasons is the strongest.

I have already said why and in what measure I am a Peronista because of his cause. May I say how and in what measure I am a Peronista because of him, because of him personally?

At this juncture, perhaps it might be convenient for those who think a "political marriage" took place between me and Perón to turn over the page.

Those who believe this happened will find here only propaganda.

✳We got married because we loved one another, and we loved one another because we both loved the same thing. In different ways we had both wanted to do the same thing: he with intelligence, I with the heart; he, prepared for the fray; I, ready for everything without knowing anything; he cultured and I simple; he great and I small; he master and I pupil.

He the figure and I the shadow.

He sure of himself, and I sure only of him!

That is why we married, even before the decisive battle for the liberty of our people, with the absolute certainty that neither triumph nor defeat, neither glory nor failure, could destroy the unity of our hearts.

Yes, I was sure of him!

I knew that power would not dazzle him nor change him.

That he would continue to be as he was: sober, smooth, an

41

early riser, insatiable in his thirst for justice, simple and humble; that he would never be otherwise than as I knew him—giving his large, warm hand generously and frankly to the men of my people.

I knew that drawing rooms would be superfluous for him, because there are too many lies told in them for a man of his caliber to endure.

Neither did I ignore what my behavior would have to be like to harmonize with his.

I knew that to harmonize with him I needed to scale very high peaks. But I was also aware of his marvelous humility in coming down to my level.

I am not ashamed to admit that I seriously intended that he should see one fault less in me each day till none remained.

How could I wish and do anything else, knowing, as I knew, his designs and plans?

For he did not win me with fair and elegant words nor with formal and high-sounding promises. He did not promise me glory or greatness or honors. Nothing marvelous.

Indeed, I believe he never promised me anything! Speaking of the future, he always talked to me only of his people, and I ended by convincing myself that his promise of love lay there, among his people, among my people. Among our people!

It is the path which all we women take when we love a man with a cause.

First, the cause is "his cause." Then we begin to call it "my cause." And when love reaches its greatest perfection, the feeling of admiration that made us say "his cause," and the selfish feeling that made us say "my cause," are superseded by a feeling of complete unity, and we say "our cause."

When that moment comes, it is impossible to say whether love for the cause is greater or less than love for the man of that cause. I think the two things are in reality one.

That is why I say now: "Yes, I am Peronista, fanatically Peronista!" But I would not be able to say which I love most, Perón or his cause, for to me it is all one and the same thing, it is all one love; and when I say in my speeches and in my conversation that Perón is the nation and is the people, I do no more than prove that everything in my life is sealed by one single love.

13

Apprenticeship

MAY I GO on talking about Perón?

Although some may say—and how it has been said!—that it is neither in good taste nor intelligent of me, I have to go on praising my Leader.

Who could do it as well? I know him, being his wife and a Peronista; I know him in his calling as President and in his home life; I know how he works and how he rests, when he speaks and when he is silent, how he enjoys himself and how he suffers. I know his smallest gestures, those little gestures that spring only from great souls.

I would be disloyal to my people if I did not speak of him. On the other hand, nobody can think my praise other than disinterested.

I have already received from him all I could hope for—much more than I deserve.

And it is not through gratitude, either, that I always speak of him, everywhere, in all my speeches and in all my conversation, without exception. I speak of him simply through necessity, for the same reason that poets make verses, and the roses bloom.

I remember, for example, how he went on teaching me his doctrine, showing me his plans, acquainting me with the great

45

problems of national life; and how he made me distinguish between what was possible and impossible, the ideal and the practical.

Each talk with him is a marvelous lesson that never seems like a lesson.

Not only do I, his most constant pupil, say so. All who, for any reason, come near him, say it also.

He knows how to speak simply about the most simple things and also about the most complicated. For him there is nothing that cannot be explained in some way, even to those who know least, and he always manages to do so. No one is bored or tired by him, no one is made to feel uncomfortable. Many persons enter his office with a certain reasonable apprehension, but, after his first words, his first greeting, no longer see in him the President, the Leader of millions of men and women; he appears to all as a friend, amiable and cordial.

He is always thus. In this fashion, amiable and cordial, making me almost think that *I* was teaching *him*, he made me understand all that it was necessary for me to know in order to accomplish my mission.

⟡From him I learned, for example, to put aside all negative things, and always look for things to do, for new ideas.

Very often things have happened as follows: I have an idea which I feel is productive and useful and which, when realized, will benefit the cause of the people. When I explain it, first to a few people, generally friends, almost all approve, even if perhaps they do not all think that it is the best thing to do. But those are never lacking who quite loyally try to persuade me that it will not suit me, and so I find out that all of them, or the great majority, consider that perhaps it will not prove expedient. Sometimes they are right, but when I am absolutely convinced, when I *feel* clearly that the idea must be successful, I venture to carry it out in spite of all predictions; and such ideas have proved the best achievements of my life.

Thus the *Fundación*[1] was born. Thus arose the Peronista

[1] *Fundación* Eva Perón, the organization founded by Eva Perón to assist on a

Feminine Movement.

I learned from Perón to get off the beaten track into the region which nobody has ventured to explore.

From him I also learned to accomplish things. He is always constructive, in his conversation as well as in his actions.

He is always telling me, "One must not forget that the best is the enemy of good." And he, who always speaks so fervently of his doctrine, never forgets to add: "A great doctrine is worthless if it has no one to carry it out."

I confess I suffer from a permanent fever to accomplish things, and that it is a contagious fever.

He has taught me that to achieve things it is not necessary, as the majority of people think, to make great plans. If the plans exist, so much the better; but if not, the important thing is to commence the work and then make the plans.

So that people who think this a sin against the art of governing shall not get a wrong impression, however, I hasten to tell them that Perón is the first Argentine who has governed the country according to a premeditated plan.

From Perón I learned to deal with men.

But in this matter I acknowledge that I possess some defects. Although I am not really convinced hat they are defects.

He never expects too much from men; he is satisfied with very little. He always trusts them, without exception, as long as he has no proof of their deceitful ways. That is why the failing he most despises and which hurts him most in his friends or in his collaborators is untruthfulness.

I, on the other hand, demand much more from those who are my friends or immediate collaborators.

I own that, above all, I cannot have any beside me, working with me, except those in whom I believe and whom I fully trust. And in this I have seldom been mistaken.

I remember someone once asked me: "Why did you trust me the first time you spoke to me?"

---

large scale the needy and destitute of the land, and even extend its help to other countries in the case of such catastrophes as earthquakes and floods.

I did not know how to give a reasonable reply. Had I told the truth I should have answered: "Because I *felt* it was possible to trust you."

Often, unfortunately, the opposite happens. Sometimes I distrust too frequently. This may be due to the fact that a great part of my main duty consists of guarding the flank of a man and of a cause.

There is much intuition in this matter of knowing men. And as the subject is worthy of it and also pleases me, I want to afford it a separate chapter.

14

Intuition?

THIS MATTER OF intuition attracts me because I have often heard mine praised; and although I do not often stop to think of praise, it has been given so frequently to my intuition that sometimes I have wondered about the subject.

Here are my explanations, which do not attempt so much to explain a psychological problem—which is beyond me—as to say frankly what I think.

I believe it is not a sixth sense, as some say, nor an almost mysterious power belonging to woman, as others claim.

No; it is simply a form of intelligence, different in each one. In some it works quickly, in others it is slow.

Everyone looks on things according to what he wishes to see in them. I always remember the old proverb which says: "Objects are the color of the glasses through which we view them."

When people wish to attribute "intuition" to women as a mysterious virtue, they forget we have to look in a special way at things, at persons and at life.

⚹We feel, and we suffer from love, more than men. Our intelligence develops in the shelter of the heart, and that is why our intelligence is not evident except through the glasses of love.

And love, whose mystery is indeed infinite, makes our intelligence see things it could never discern by itself, however clever.

Men do not feel or suffer so much through love as women. This requires no proof.

In them intelligence grows freely.

And because of that they see everything by cold logic, almost mathematically, and the more coldly and mathematically the less they have felt, or suffered from love.

When some people praise my "intuition," they always refer to the way I get to know the persons with whom I have to deal.

Sometimes I have trusted those who were distrusted by many, and at other times I have distrusted those in whom all believed.

Nearly always, time has proved me right.

Is this a mysterious virtue? I do not think so. On the contrary, it all seems to me very simple. I have always regarded people in a special way. I look through very fine glasses: those of love for Perón and for his cause.

Love lengthens the range of vision of the intelligence.

If it were not so, how could I feel "intuitively" so many things which often I do not quite understand?

I remember one night when I went to bed very late and could not sleep.

I was worried by a national problem whose solution had already been proposed to the President by government experts.

I had spoken to no one about it, and knew nothing except what was published in the newspapers.

It was a serious and difficult problem which I had never even tried to understand. But I did not like the proposed solution!

The worst of it was that I did not know exactly why.

Obviously I could say next day that I did not like the solution, but I should have to give my reasons. And I could not find any!

Nor did I find them; but I decided to confide my feelings to the President; and I was right, for he, who had also been worried, thinking out the problem, was already disposed to revise the solution proposed by his collaborators.

Strange? Mysterious? No, it was the miracle of ordinary intelligence illumined by love.

There is nothing unusual, then, about this virtue or "uncommon sense" attending Perón's actions and admired by all who know him and have dealings with him.

He, who loves his people profoundly, sees everything through that great love, and consequently, as is also evident, in a special manner, different from that which guides the view of others.

He sees through his people, and for his people.

Why should it be strange, then, that, illumined by that great love, he should feel "intuitively" where the happiness of Argentines and national greatness can be found?

And I certainly can vouch for his possessing the virtue to a marvelous degree. He understands men at a glance, even though they often try to dissemble in his presence. Very often, also, I have seen him deciding serious problems in a way different from that advised by experts and specialists, and more than once when I have questioned him wonderingly I have heard him say:

"It's a matter of common sense.

"They see the problem from a technical angle, which is limited, like the field of a microscope. I have to look at it with plain glasses; I have to see it as the people see and feel it."

After pondering on this explanation, I have also thought that "common sense" and "intuition" are two virtues which have not yet been well defined and may be the same thing; I think they exist in all men and women in greater or lesser degree, and only increase and become extraordinary when a great love breathes life into them through the wonderful strength of its infinite power.

What I am also sure of is that no "ordinary man" can do or

think anything through "intuition"; because the average man belongs to a class that despises love as an exaggeration.

15

The Path I Chose

WHEN PERON ARRIVED at the presidency, he became convinced little by little that the responsibilities and tasks of his office were almost incompatible with his wish to maintain close contact with the people.

This contact, which was and continues to be absolutely necessary, must be permanently maintained.

Our people has lived under more than a century of oligarchical governments whose principal task was not to attend to the people but rather to the interests of a privileged minority, refined and cultured perhaps, but sordidly egoistic.

After that century, interrupted only by someone or other who tried to establish a government for the people, or, rather, by some effort or other never converted into reality, Perón during three years of revolutionary fire reached the people as governor and as guide. And the people already knew how that contact had benefited everyone.

For three consecutive years, men and women, labor, economic and political groups, the entire people, had come in procession with their old problems and their old hopes into the constructive presence of their Leader, and all their problems and all their hopes had been satisfactorily settled by him as far as was possible—and perhaps even a little further.

With Perón in the presidency with a fullness of power extra-ordinary in Argentina, how would not the hopes and illusions of people who had already known the taste of a "government of the people . . . for the people" be doubled?

But it was precisely the fullness of power which would prevent the Leader from having permanent contact with the people. While he was at the Secretariat of Labor and Welfare he had no other problems to settle but the old and urgent problems directly affecting the people. But in the presidency, the old and urgent problems were others whose solution was indispensable if all he had accomplished in three years of social reform was not to fall to the ground. What would have been the use of three years of revolution if at the end of the war we had fallen anew into the arms of our traditional imperialistic exploiters?

Would social reform have been of any use to us in a country without riches and without work, delivered with bound hands to the foreign will of international capitalism?

All this Perón saw clearer than ever from the day he became President; and so that it should not happen, he had to devote himself entirely to achieving his main goal, which was nothing less than the economic independence of the nation.

In four months he elaborated his five-year-plan of government.

In two years he had brought about economic independence. But I do not want to say just how much the General did as President, although I would gladly write an unending number of pages on this inexhaustible subject.

What is certain is that all this immense task, which had to commence with organizing the very government itself, and whose first stage culminated with the reform of the Constitution, could leave him only limited time for maintaining his contact with the people.

And if we had not searched together for a solution, and found it, the voice of the people—that of our *descamisados*—would have reached the seat of government with ever duller accent, and perhaps might have been hushed altogether.

On the other hand, it was necessary to keep the revolutionary fervor kindled in the people. The revolution was hardly under way, and Perón had to cover all its stages from the government itself. This could be done, but only if the people maintained their revolutionary fervor and were not won over by the teachings of the "ordinary men," to whom all revolutionary action seems an unpardonable indiscretion.

Between the decree of the law of the revolution and its accomplishment, and between the government and the people, numerous barriers always exist which are not always seen from the government, but which are clearly visible to the people. Contact between Perón and the people was necessary also for this fundamental reason.

In addition, there were urgent though modest tasks to be done concerning the daily needs of the humble. Among the hopes of the *descamisados* were many little illusions which they brought to Perón just as children do to their parents.

The requests and wants of each family vary greatly. The grownups want important things, the children ask for toys. In the great family consisting of the nation, the requests presented to the President, who is the common father, are also infinite.

We were already aware of this when Perón was President-elect. The hopes of the people took the form of the most varied petitions, from a government undertaking of extraordinary and even fantastic nature urged by a whole town, to a football wanted by a "little monkey" from the north, or a doll which a little Indian girl desired.

And to attend to all this—big things and small—it was necessary that the people should not leave off looking to Perón as their guide.

I chose the humble task of attending to small petitions.

I chose my place among the people so as to see from there the barriers which might have hindered the progress of the revolution.

I chose to be "Evita" . . . so that through me the people, and above all the workers, should always find the way open to their Leader.

The solution could not have been better or more practicable.

Problems of government reach Perón every day through his ministers, from public officials or from those themselves concerned; but each one of them cannot take up more than a few minutes in the exhausting day of a President like Perón.

On the other hand, the people's problems reach the Leader every day during lunch or supper, on calm Saturday afternoons, on long, quiet Sundays, and they reach him through my voice, loyal and frank, under suitable circumstances, when the soul of the General is free from all pressing worries.

Thus the people may be sure that no separation is possible between them and their government. Because in the case of Argentina, in order to divorce himself from his people, the head of the government would have to begin by divorcing his own wife!

16
Eva Perón and "Evita"

THERE IS IN my destiny nothing extraordinary, and even less that is due to chance.

I cannot say I think all that has happened to me is logical and reasonable, but I would not be sincere if I did not say that it all seems to me at least natural.

I have already set forth the principal causes of the mission which it has fallen to my lot to accomplish in my country. My explanation would not be complete, however, if I did not say something also about the circumstances which made me decide to bring myself into strict collaboration with General Perón after he became President of the Argentines.

Before starting on the subject, it is well to remember that Perón is not only President of the Republic; he is also the Leader of his people.

This is a fundamental condition, and is directly related to my decision to handle the role of wife to the President of the Republic in a manner different from any President's wife who had preceded me.

I could have followed in the old pattern. I want to make this very clear, because people have also wished to explain my "incomprehensible sacrifice" by arguing that the drawing rooms of the oligarchy would have been closed to me in any event.

Nothing is further than this from all reality, nor more remote from all common sense.

I might have been a President's wife like the others.

It is a simple and agreeable role: a holiday job, the task of receiving honors, of decking oneself out to go through the motions prescribed by social dictates. It is all very similar to what I was able to do previously, and I think more or less successfully, in the theater and in the cinema.

As for the hostility of the oligarchy, I can only smile.

And I wonder: why would the oligarchy have been able to reject me?

Because of my humble origin? Because of my artistic career?

But has that class of person ever bothered about these things here—or in any part of the world—when it was a case of the wife of a President?

The oligarchy has never been hostile to anyone who could be useful to it. Power and money were never bad antecedents to a genuine oligarch.

The truth is different. I, who had learned from Perón to choose unusual paths, did not wish to follow the old pattern of wife of the President.

Also, anyone who knows me a bit—I don't mean now, but from before, when I was a "simple Argentine girl"—knows that I could never have enacted the cold comedy of oligarchical drawing rooms.

I was not born for that. On the contrary, there was always in my soul an open repugnance for that kind of acting.

But also, I was not only the wife of the President of the Republic, I was also the wife of the Leader of the Argentines.

I had to have a double personality to correspond with Perón's double personality. One, Eva Perón, wife of the President, whose work is simple and agreeable, a holiday job of receiving honors, of gala performances; the other, "Evita," wife of the Leader of a people who have placed all their faith in him, all their hope and all their love.

A few days of the year I act the part of Eva Perón; and I think

I do better each time in that part, for it seems to me to be neither difficult nor disagreeable.

The immense majority of days I am, on the other hand, "Evita," a link stretched between the hopes of the people and the fulfilling hands of Perón, Argentina's first woman Peronista —and this indeed is a difficult role for me, and one in which I am never quite satisfied with myself.

There is no need for us to speak of Eva Perón.

What she does appear too lavishly in the newspapers and reviews everywhere.

On the other hand, it is interesting for us to talk about "Evita"; not because I feel at all vain about being she, but because those who understand "Evita" may find it easy afterward to understand her *descamisados*, the people themselves, who will never feel themselves more important than they are . . . and so will never turn into an oligarchy, which, in the eyes of a Peronista, is the worst thing that can happen.

17

"Evita"

WHEN I CHOSE to be "Evita," I chose the path of my people.

Now, four years after that choice, it is easy for me to prove that this was certainly so.

Only the people call me "Evita." Only the *descamisados* learned to call me so. Men of the government, political leaders, ambassadors, men of business, professional men, intellectuals, etc., who call on me usually address me as "Señora"; and some of these address me publicly as "Most Excellent Señora" or "Most Worthy Señora," and even, at times, as "Señora Presidenta."

They see in me only Eva Perón.

The *descamisados*, on the other hand, know me only as "Evita."

I appeared to them thus the day I went to meet the humble of my land, telling them that I preferred being "Evita" to being the wife of the President, if that "Evita" could help to mitigate some grief, or dry a tear.

If a man of the government, a leader, a politician, an ambassador, who normally calls me "Señora," should call me "Evita," it would sound as strange and out of place to me as if a street-urchin, a workingman or a humble person of the people should call me "Señora."

But I think it would seem still stranger to him!

Now, if you ask me which I prefer, my reply would be immediately that I prefer the name by which I am known to the people.

When a street-urchin calls me "Evita," I feel as though I were the mother of all the urchins, and of all the weak and the humble of my land.

When a workingman calls me "Evita," I feel glad to be the companion of all the workingmen of my country and even of the whole world.

When a woman of my country calls me "Evita," I imagine myself her sister, and that of all the women of humanity.

And so, almost without noticing it, I have classified in these three examples the principal activities of "Evita" relating to the humble, the workers and women.

The truth is that, without any artificial effort, at no personal cost, as though I had been born for all this, I feel myself responsible for the humble as though I *were* the mother of all of them; I fight shoulder to shoulder with the workers as though I *were* another of their companions from the workshop or factory; in front of the women who trust in me, I consider myself something like an elder sister, responsible to a certain degree for the destiny of all of them who have placed their hopes in me.

And certainly I do not deem this an honor but a responsibility.

I believe that every one of the men and the women forming the mass of humanity should feel at least a bit responsible for all the rest. Perhaps then we would all be a little happier!

I attend to the trade-union problems of the workingmen.

I receive from the humble those complaints and needs which are not related to the State, even though at times in these cases I also act as the government's diligent collaborator. In the end it is all grist for the mill of our common Leader.

I attend to women's problems in their multiple social, cultural and political aspects.

If anyone should ask me which of my activities I prefer, I would not be able to answer with precision.

If the question were put to me when engaged in trade-union matters, my choice would be for these. If I were attending to my *descamisados* or to women, perhaps I would vote for the matter on which I was engaged at that very moment. And I would not do so through "diplomacy" or "politics." No! But because, when I am working, what I am doing at the moment seems to me best, the most to my taste, to my vocation and to my liking.

I realize, though, that at the bottom what I like most is to be with the people in their most genuine forms: the workers, the humble, the women . . .

With them I do not need to pose at all, as I sometimes have to when I am Eva Perón. I speak and feel as they do, simply and frankly, sometimes smoothly and sometimes roughly, but always loyally.

We never fail to understand one another. On the other hand, sometimes Eva Perón is not wont to understand those attending functions at which she must be present.

Do not think by this that "Evita's" work comes easily to me. Rather, it always turns out to be difficult, and I have never felt quite satisfied in that role. On the other hand, the part of Eva Perón seems easy. And it is not strange. For is it not always easier to act a stage part than to live it in person?

And in my case, it is certainly as Eva Perón that I interpret an ancient role which other women in all ages have already lived; but as "Evita" I live a reality which perhaps no woman has lived in the history of humanity.

I have said that I am guided by no personal ambition. And perhaps that isn't quite true.

Yes. I confess that I have an ambition, one single, great personal ambition: I would like the name of "Evita" to figure somewhere in the history of my country.

I would like it to be said of her, even if only in a small footnote to the marvelous chapter which history will certainly devote to Perón, something more or less like this:

"There was, at Perón's side, a woman who dedicated herself to conveying to the President the hopes of the people which later Perón converted into realities."

And I would feel duly compensated—and more—if the note ended like this:

"All we know about that woman is that the people called her, fondly, *Evita*."

18

Small Details

ALL THAT I have to do between the people and their Leader demands a condition that I have had to take infinite care to comply with. That is, not to interfere in matters of government.

Neither would it be tolerated by the President, who because of his military training has his opinions on responsibility and jurisdiction.

Often, however, I have to tell the people, face to face, what I would tell their Leader, and consequently I have also to tell the Leader what the people want to reach his ear.

And this duty leads me at times to discuss with the General subjects which appertain to the government. In these cases I never forget that I have chosen to be on the side of the people.

Doubtless the men of the government should be sufficient for Perón in the accomplishment of his work, but it is not useless, I think, for the voice of a person identified with him and with his cause to reach him daily with fresh news of the people whom he loves so deeply.

Perhaps the only good I do, fulfilling thus my humble mission, is to cheer his soul with the words and the affections of his people which I confide in his heart while he rests from his tasks.

I do not worry about lack of precedent. On the contrary, it

gladdens and comforts me. And while the "ordinary men," those of always despicable mediocrity, poisonous and sterile, search only for new ways in which to attack, our movement offers them daily something unprecedented, something original which belongs exclusively to us.

I know that when they criticize my part in the movement, what really hurts them at heart is the revolution.

My contact with the people hurts them. They know that while that contact is unbroken—and it will not be broken by me!—the people can reach Perón, and Perón will perform his duty to his people.

While this can happen, the "ordinary men" will not get back into power.

That is why they try to destroy me.

They know also that I do not work for myself. They will never see me looking for personal gain, and that incites them.

They would like me to succumb to egoism and ambition so as to prove to the people that in the people I looked only for my own interests.

They know that in this way they could separate me from the people. They do not understand that in my eagerness I look for nothing but the triumph of Perón and of his cause, because the victory belongs to the people themselves.

Not even when I approach those who work, or those who suffer, do I do it because of the selfish satisfaction of one making some personal sacrifice.

I endeavor every day to eliminate from my soul sentimentality toward those who ask of me.

I do not want to be ashamed of myself in their presence. I set about my work fulfilling my duty and to satisfy justice.

No song-and-dance, no verbosity, no farces, no posing, no romanticism.

Not even when I am with the neediest can anyone say that I act the Lady Bountiful who leaves her comforts for a moment so as to imagine that she is engaged on a mission of mercy.

From Perón himself, who is always wont to say: "Love is the only constructive thing," I have learned what a work of love is, and how it should be accomplished.

Love is not—according to the lesson I have learned—either sentimental romance or a literary pretense.

Love is giving oneself, and to give oneself is to give one's own life.

If one does not give one's own life, anything one may do is only justice. When one begins to give one's own life, then only is one performing a work of love.

I do not claim by this to perform charitable works that seem to me too near to God. I content myself with helping forward the fulfillment of social justice. That is why I have given the name of "social help" to my fraternal work of assistance to the poor, and I believe it is deeply justicialist.

That is why there is no place in it for excesses of the heart. As it is a work of justice, I know that I should fulfill it in the same way as a judge administers it: as one who accomplishes a mission that has been entrusted to him, and nothing more.

Amiably certainly, but not with boasting.

This is just a detail, but I am sure it has saved me many unnecessary humiliations.

And no one can gain happiness by exchanging riches—not even all the riches of the world—for humiliation which may destroy his dignity. For dignity is man's most precious treasure.

PART TWO
The Workers
and My
Mission

19
The Secretariat

NEARLY ALL MY social welfare work is carried out at the Secretariat of Labor and Welfare, in which I occupy a small sector. I attend to my work in the same office which was Colonel Perón's from 1943 to 1945.

All this has a very special significance.

Even when the Justicialist Constitution converted the Secretariat into the Ministry of Labor and Welfare, the workers continued to call it, as in the Colonel's days, the "Secretariat." Neither do I ever call it a Ministry.

This little detail shows that the people still feel Perón's presence there.

There his vigorous personality as Leader came into contact with the people. There he convinced his first disciples. There he enjoyed his first successes. There he reaffirmed his irrevocable decision to serve the people with all his energies and above all sacrifice!

To all of us he is still in the old "Secretariat," as in the hour of his intensest struggles.

It was not through romantic oversentimentality that I chose to work there. I went to the Secretariat of Labor and Welfare because it was easiest for me to meet the people and their problems there; because the Minister of Labor and Welfare is a working man, and "Evita" gets on with him frankly and without bureaucratic red tape; and also because it was there I was offered the requisite means for commencing my work.

There I receive the workers, the humble, those who need me for any personal or collective problem.

Its officials collaborate with me in the solving of trade-union problems, collecting all the antecedents, examining them on their own merits and for their economic and social repercussions.

As regards my works of social help, I also carry them out at the Secretariat, but its staff has only to deal with a few details connected with requests for audiences.

Problems of the feminine political movement do not take up my time at the Secretariat, since I prefer to attend to these at the headquarters of the Feminine Peronista Party or at our private residence.

Attending to the workers takes up almost all the time I give to audiences and to my work at the Secretariat. This is a natural requirement of the Peronista movement, whose history and whose realization have been accomplished thanks to the total support of the organized workers of my country.

I am prone to hear it said to the President that governments and States are leaving behind the period when everything was decided through the functioning of political organizations, and progressing to the period when all is decided through the functioning of social organizations.

And the Peronista government, inspired by its leader, tries to be in the van and relies more and more on trade-union organizations.

I think (with Perón's vision and judgment to inspire me) that the people are almost always better represented today by trade-union organizations than by political parties.

Political parties frequently fall into the power of cliques of leaders kept in office thanks to negotiations and compromises which are not always quite apparent. This does not happen with trade-union organizations, whose leaders must live in contact with the masses they represent if they do not wish to disappear from the directive scene.

I can say quite frankly, from my four years' experience, that the trade-union leaders are better acquainted with the people's realities than are the political leaders.

And to tell the truth, I must also say that political leaders excel trade-union leaders only when they know how to maintain honest contact with the trade-union organizations. By "honest contact" I mean that maintained by those political leaders who work loyally for the workers' cause without intention, either overt or hidden, of using them as a medium for their personal ambitions.

In the Secretariat I learned all I know about syndicalism and labor problems.

There I found everything already in operation: a method and a technique for dealing with the resolving of trade-union problems—the method and technique of Colonel Perón. I have done nothing but follow in his footsteps, guided by his example, and very often I have had recourse to his advice as master and guide.

Only thus have I been able to succeed in making the Secretariat continue to function as the home of the Argentine workers, as Colonel Perón intended and shaped it in the first days of his struggle.

20

A Superior Presence

FROM THE WATCHTOWER of the Secretariat one can see the entire panorama of Argentina trade-unionism. I, who saw it in 1944 and 1945 from a corner of the same office of which I am now the head, in the days when Colonel Perón was wont to allow me to watch him work, can only say, perhaps, how everything has changed in this sector of my country.

Until 1943 the workers' claims in Argentina had a doctrine and technique which differed in no wise from the doctrine and technique of the rest of the countries of the world.

This doctrine and technique were international—that is to say, foreign in all countries and to all peoples, because when a thing is international it loses the right to call itself national even in the country of its origin.

The leaders of the claims of Argentine workers had been shaped in that doctrine, and they had been taught that technique and that only.

I will not say that they were altogether bad leaders, nor do I wish to fall into the error of even thinking that they did not genuinely represent their companions. On the contrary, I think they did their duty honestly, as well as they were able, for the masses who put their confidence in them. Or, rather, their despair!—because in the face of the brutal selfishness of the capitalistic and relentless oligarchy, what else but desperation could the working masses have in electing their leaders? That is why they often preferred to elect those who proposed more radical and extreme measures theoretically, than to hand the direction over to those who would have been able to demand and achieve some practical and immediate benefit, however small.

This explains why—elected by the desperation of the working masses who were suffering, and inspired by hatred—these trade-union leaders, powerless to satisfy those they represented, found themselves obliged to sidetrack the masses' attentions to problems of international politics, using highflown propaganda to expound doctrines foreign to the real and pressing needs of the people.

But the leaders' great defect did not consist in this, which, after all, they were almost obliged by circumstances to do. The great sin was that often they thought, spoke and acted in a language strange to their companions, ignoring home realities. They did not understand (for I do not think they acted in bad faith, at least not the majority) that the problem of the Argentine workers had very little to do with the problem of the workers in the Old World, overpopulated, with no kind of economic reserves.

They did not gauge Argentine realities aright.

Some, perhaps the highest leaders of those times, did *not* proceed, however, in good faith.

Just as I recognize that the majority acted with a high conception of the trade-union spirit, I must also say that some were betrayers of the working masses.

And in saying this I do not think I am saying anything new to Argentine workers.

All of them remember how these supposed labor leaders allied themselves in shady union with the rankest oligarchy, and, under the protection of the conservative and capitalistic press, which plotted against the Argentines, attempted the destruction of the Leader in 1946.

With this they proved that the enmity feigned in the face of capitalism by communists and socialists, who for so long called themselves the leaders of "the people," was a lie.

This also explains why for so many years Argentine workers did not see their organizations progress except by slow stages, and these only occasionally and with bloody and painful sacrifice.

But it is not of these false labor leaders, now definitely allied to the oligarchy, that I wish to speak. It is the others, those of good faith and true trade-union spirit, about whom I want to write a bit more.

I have already said that until 1943 they lived a doctrine and technique of strife. They believed firmly that this was the best, and even the only, road by which to attain their dreamed-of well-being. Only when Perón told them from the Secretariat of Labor and Welfare of another technique did they begin to understand the error which had lost them many years and so much effort.

At first the Colonel disconcerted them.

For fifty years they had heard high leaders speak against the nation, and consequently against the army. And now a military man, an "obscure colonel"—the oligarchy said—claimed to show them which path was the one of justice and happiness.

To crown all, the new Leader spoke to them of the spirit and of its values, not preaching of the struggle between capital and labor, but rather of co-operation, and even told them that it was necessary to put the old, forgotten principles of Christianity into practice.

How could they not be disconcerted?

But, little by little, they came to believe in the Colonel. Many believed only through hearing him, others when they could see him.

The majority believed when his promises began to come true.

And so the honest leaders of Argentine syndicalism allied themselves to Perón. On the opposite side remained those who did not want to hear the promises or want to see the facts. They had already sold their places in advance to the oligarchy and to capitalism. But in exchange for this, they were forgotten by the workers—forgotten in the way the people have of scorning those who betray them.

Perón's technique asserted itself in two years of restless struggles. Once he was in the presidency, however, there was the danger that some indignant "specialists" in syndicalism might try to regroup the workers with the old rhetoric and the old ideas so well studied by them in the foreign school which had shaped them . . . and paid them; and to this end they might endeavor to represent the Secretariat as simply one more government office, cold and bureaucratic after the style of the old National Department of Labor, which in 1943 had acquired the total and absolute contempt of the Argentine workers.

It might also have happened that, with the genial creator of the new doctrine and the new technique for labor recovery absent from the Secretariat, the leaders themselves—even the Peronistas—dominated unconsciously or infiltrated by others, might have returned to the old doctrine and the old methods.

The presence of an old trade-union leader at the head of the Ministry of Labor and Welfare was the first step to avoid that happening. But it was insufficient, in view of the fact that his presence inspired only confidence: confidence in a companion and in a friend. To avoid the danger, something more was necessary. And I think that something more was and continues to be my presence, not so much because of what I am worth or can do, but because I am too close to the Leader for a little of his magnificent presence not to accompany me wherever I am.

When we see someone's shadow, we feel that he is near. Thus my presence at the Secretariat is as the shadow of the Leader. And in his shadow I intend to continue along the path he started. I know there is a great difference. Where he gave a masterly lesson, I hardly babble. Where he solved a problem in four words, I am sometimes stuck for a week at a time. Where he decided, I suggest. Where he saw light, I hardly see a glimmer. It is he who is the guide. I am only the shadow of his superior presence.

21
The Workers and I

MY WORK FOR the workers has a very simple technique, although at times the problems brought to me are complicated and difficult.

I have already said that, in spite of it, I feel at ease among them, and that we always end by understanding one another.

Sometimes people ask me what I am to the workers of my country. I prefer to explain first what the workers are to me.

To me the workingmen and working women are always, and above all, *descamisados*.

And what do the *descamisados* mean to me? I cannot speak of them without recalling my days of loneliness in October, 1945.

It is impossible to define a *descamisado* without turning back to those days, just as it is impossible perhaps to explain light without thinking of the sun.

The *descamisados* are all those who were in the Plaza de Mayo[1] on the 17th of October, 1945; those who swam across the Riachuelo coming from Avellaneda, the Boca and the Province of Buenos Aires; those who in happy columns, though ready for anything, including death, marched that unforgettable day along the Avenida de Mayo and by the diagonal avenues leading to Government House and silenced the oligarchy and him

[1]The historic square in front of Government House.

who said "I am not Perón"; those who all day long clamored with shouts for the presence of the absent and captive Leader; those who lit bonfires with the newspapers of the press that had sold itself to a foreign ambassador for thirty pieces of silver, or perhaps less!

All those who were in the Plaza de Mayo that night were *descamisados*!

Even if someone was there who was not, materially speaking, a *descamisado*, he gained that title for having felt and suffered that night with all those genuine *descamisados*; and to me he was and always will be an authentic *descamisado*.

And all those who then, had they been there, would have gone to the Plaza de Mayo; and all those who today or tomorrow would do the same as those first *descamisados* of that first 17th of October, are *descamisados*.

That is why to me a *descamisado* is *he who feels himself of the people*. What is important is this: that he feel himself to be of the people, that he love and suffer and enjoy with the people—even if he does not dress the part, for that is of no consequence.

An oligarch who has come down in the world may be materially a *descamisado*, but he will not be a genuine *descamisado*.

At this point I declare myself an enemy of the concept established by Peronista doctrine.

To me the workers are, because of this, in the first place *descamisados*: they were all in the Plaza de Mayo that night. Many were there in person; all were there in spirit.

Not all *descamisados* are workingmen, but to me every workingman is a *descamisado*; and I shall never forget that I owe a little of Perón's life to each *descamisado*.

In the second place, they are an integral part of the people: of that people whose cause won my heart many years ago.

And in the third place, they are the powerful forces upholding the scaffolding on whose framework the very building of the revolution is erected.

The Peronista movement could not be defined without them.

General Perón has said that justicialism would not be possible without syndicalism. And this is true, first, because General Perón has said so, and secondly, because it is actually the truth.

In reality the syndicalism of my country is actually the most powerful organizing force supporting the Peronista movement.

More than four million workers are grouped in the General Confederation of Labor alone, which is the labor center; all have united in determining in favor of Perón's justicialist doctrine.

That is why each worker is also to me a genuine Peronista: the best of all the Peronistas, because he is also "the people," and in addition a *descamisado*.

The workers who come to my office with their hopes, with their illusions and with their problems, mean all this to me.

When I find myself with them, what should I be except a companion or a friend?—a companion whose undying gratitude cannot be expressed except in one way: with absolute and deepest loyalty!

And they know it well; they know I am not the State, and much less the master.

That is why they are wont to say: "Evita is tough, but she is loyal."

They know I have only one price, which is the love of my people. For love of my people—and they are the people!—I would sell all I am and have, and I think I would also give my life.

They know that when I tell them to "go easy" I do so for their own good, just as when I spur them on in the struggle.

As time goes on, that confidence grows firmer in our movement, for every day I give them proof of my loyalty. And the confidence they have in me is increasingly greater, to such a point that they have hope in me even when everything seems lost.

It often happens that a labor problem, either because it has been badly conducted or through insoluble economic difficulties, cannot be settled to the satisfaction of the workers. That is when my work, instead of being plain and simple, becomes difficult. That is when I try hardest to find a solution, and my greatest joy is to discover it and offer it to the workers.

Was it not they who found the seemingly hopeless solution to a problem when they regained Perón for themselves—and for me—on the 17th of October, 1945?

And when my resources are exhausted, then we have recourse to the supreme resource, which is Perón's fullness of power—he in whose hands all hope, even though it be but a forlorn hope, is transformed into reality.

22

Only One Class of Men

AT THIS STAGE I must repeat a lesson that I have often heard from the General.

It pertains to the justicialist concept of work and capital, which serves as a basis for my work of trade-union character.

The fundamental object of justicialism in relation to the workers' movement is to end class war and substitute co-operation between capital and labor.

Capitalism—to give everything to capital—exploits the workers.

Communism, to solve this problem, proposes a system of strife which is not to end until there is only one social class; but this one-class society is to be attained through destruction—a long struggle, without quarter, between capital and labor.

Justicialism, on the other hand, also wishes to arrive at a single class: those who work. This is one of the real fundamentals of Peronism. But it wishes to achieve this end by co-operation rather than strife.

We do not want a single proletariat class, but a single class of *former* proletarians who will live and work worthily.

Our aim is that the workers earn enough to live honestly, like human beings, and that the masters also be content to gain enough to maintain industry and progress and live worthily.

Worthily, but not like princes!

We do not want anyone to exploit anyone, and that is all. This is what Perón has tried to assure for his people, and this objective has remained well established in the new Constitution.

I, however, because of my nature, am not always in accord with this strict balance of justice. I recognize it. Almost always justice for me is a little farther than the middle of the road . . . nearer to the workers than to the masters!

The problem is this: in order to attain the only class of Argentines that Perón wants, the workers must still rise a bit more; but the masters have a long way to come down.

What is certain is that I, who see in each worker a *descamisado* and a Peronista, cannot see the same, unless it is well proved, in a master.

I am a sectarian; that is true. I do not deny it; I have, indeed, affirmed it. But, can anyone deny me that right? Can the workers be denied the humble privilege of having me more on their side than on that of their masters—when it was they, and they only, during my bitter Calvary of 1945, who opened their doors to me and held out a friendly hand?

My sectarianism is also a compensation and an atonement. For a century the privileged class was the exploiter of the working class. To counterbalance this injustice, another century is needed during which the privileged class shall be the workers!

Only when this century is over will the moment have come to mete out the same measure to the workers as to the masters; although I suspect that by then justicialism will have attained its ideal of a single class: those who work.

I do not aspire to be a prophet, but I am firmly convinced that, when this century is over, men will remember Perón's name with affection, and they will bless him for having taught them how to live.

23

Condescend

SOME ARE APT to think—and they have even told me so candidly —that in dealing with the workers I am making too great and too generous a sacrifice.

More than once, above all at the commencement of my work, when my visitors did not know my "replies," the word "condescend" was pronounced in my presence.

"You condescend generously to the workers," they said.

Or, by way of counsel:

"Perhaps it would not be suitable for you to make the great sacrifice of condescending to them."

I know that at times one indignant look was sufficient for an answer.

At other times indignation went as far as words themselves, and I recognize that in this I was hard, including my remarks to a few friends who did not understand me.

I neither sacrifice myself nor condescend.

Nothing in my dealing with the workers is disagreeable to me.

They are simple men; that is so. They say things crudely, I agree. They do not hedge about to say what they think, for they have not yet learned to lie. When I have not made good on some occasion they have even told me so, and they have known how to say it without offending me.

I have never selected the workers who visit me. I know that at times even a few communists, infiltrated among the Peronistas, have come to see me. But I have never been offended by a single word.

We have had very weighty problems to discuss, and sometimes these discussions have been plain-spoken and prolonged; but I have never had to "condescend" to receive low, rough or indignant language.

All these oligarchs who think that I "condescend" by dealing with the workers would learn a lot from them, and perhaps—although I say this without any hope—might even "ascend" a little in honesty and dignity.

It is precisely in oligarchic circles that the exaggerated pretensions of the workers are wont to be spoken of.

I can assure anyone that it is quite exceptional for them to demand more than is just; when they do ask for more than is reasonable, it is due to an error in reckoning which they soon acknowledge, or to the advice of bad friends infiltrated among them, or to the masters themselves, to whom an increase of wages is often an excuse for raising prices ten times more than the increase in wages justifies.

Our workers are so sensible in the way they demand better conditions that often I have been able to "surprise" them by obtaining more for them than the most optimistic had asked for.

There is never a lack of workers in my office. I often see them speaking with the ministers, with high officials, ambassadors and illustrious and even famous visitors.

I like to see how the workers are not afraid of dealing with men of any rank, and feel themselves their equals—and why not? Sometimes, in my office, they even "feel they are higher than the others" because there they are the privileged ones.

The others can aspire to the right to my friendship; the workers know that they already have a right to a little more than my friendship—that is, my affection.

I have learned much by seeing how the workers treat and appreciate the others.

I know now that the men who are able to win the affection of the workers are generally worthy of the Peronista movement; and that those who cannot or do not know how to gain that affection are of no use for our struggle.

For the workers give their friendship and their affection only to those who honestly and faithfully offer them friendship. And they possess a fine sensibility which enables them to discover those who wish to use friendship only as a bridge for personal ambition.

I could write for days on end on the thousand smallest details of my syndicate work.

But I want only to point out what is fundamental, what will make many persons understand a little of the meaning of the work I do as an unrelinquishable duty of gratitude and of love.

Yet no one can have an exact idea of all this if he has not had the opportunity of knowing the generous and noble souls of the men whom work has dignified in its own incomparable way.

One cannot "lower oneself" to that dignity. It is as absurd as though one said: "I am going to lower myself to Aconcagua."

One can only raise oneself to that dignity, and my principal ambition is to rise a bit higher each day.

A 1945 theatrical poster featuring the emergent actress, Eva Duarte

Radiant and charming, 'Madame President' arrives at Orly Airport in July 1947 on a European tour

Two contrasting Evas: addressing a rally in the Plaza Del Mayo and receiving an award in 1952 from the Syrian government. The latter is one of the last pictures taken of the dying Evita.

Maria Eva Duarte de Perón

24

Wednesday Afternoons

EVERY WEDNESDAY AFTERNOON General Perón devotes exclusively to trade-union workers.

Government House has a special look about it on these afternoons.

Customarily, audiences of the President of the Republic are granted individually, although there is never a lack of visits from more or less numerous groups of persons.

But on Wednesday afternoons audiences are always numerous. Many delegations of workers are received, and there are many workers in each delegation.

Wednesday afternoon is, furthermore, the only afternoon in the week when my work is carried out near to the General.

Perhaps it is fitting for my readers to know some details of this work of mine.

Wednesday afternoons are to me something like afternoons of harvest.

All my work of the week gives its best fruits during the five or six hours I spend at Government House on that day.

During the week I receive from the trade-unions their requests for audiences.

Naturally, they would all like to be always visiting the President, and in this lies a little of the difficulty of my role as

"Evita."

It is in this portion of my activities that I see more clearly the reality of that humble but probably useful work for my people.

At least that is what I think.

Not all the trade-unions can see the Leader every Wednesday; but all have an equal right.

I distribute this principle very simply:

I try to arrange for each trade-union to meet the General at least once or twice a year.

Of course the only ones to hold that privilege are the higher leaders, to whom companions from the syndicate's branches in the interior of the country are often likely to be added. This generally happens each time a trade-union meets in a national assembly.

Logically, there must be an exceptional reason for each audience, since anything taking up the time of the President of the Republic should also be something exceptional.

The exceptional reason is always to be found in the life of the workers' organizations.

Sometimes it is a problem that can be settled only by Perón in his double quality of Leader of the country and of the movement.

None but he in the country holds that double investiture and that double degree of power.

There are always trade-union problems whose solutions involve not only the workers' interests but also those of the people, and even of the nationitself.

In these cases only the Leader of the workers, the guide of the people and of the nation, can see the panorama in its entirety.

Only he can make the workers see where and how far the various elements of the problem can and should be settled.

Sometimes I am likely to assist also at these audiences, and I feel happy at this confirmation of the fact that the Leader receives directly from the workers the anxieties of the people; that the people know at first hand what their guide thinks, what he wants to do and what he does.

I think there cannot be many people who thus, so simply,

without any prescribed rules whatever, can be in contact with the supreme authority of the country.

Furthermore, I think that in this lies a great part of the secret of Perón's success in the governing of the destinies of his people.

Because, at these audiences, it is not obligatory to speak only of the problem which is the motive of the interview.

The General himself asks his visitors about any problems which may be on his mind at the time, as President and Leader.

Sometimes the cost of living is spoken of, or wages in general, or international politics.

Perhaps that is why, at one time, when a matter of international anxiety hung over the country, Perón could say to the Argentines:

"I will do nothing but what the people wish."

And that was enough to calm the whole country.

The people know very well that Perón knows what his people want.

At other times trade-union audiences have as their motive the acquainting of the President with the state of the organization's activities.

All through the year, the trade-unions work for their own improvement.

Thus, for example, in addition to their efforts to better wages and working conditions, they build sanatoriums, hospitals, organize their co-operative and mutual-benefit societies, their trade-union qualifying schools, their libraries, their clubs, etc., and feel themselves happy when they can take to him who has shown them the way the results of having listened to his counsel as friend and as Leader.

At other times the object of the audience is to inform the President of the decisions taken by a national assembly of the trade-union.

Generally in these cases delegates from all the country attend, and then I also am wont to be present at the interview.

Under these circumstances we first listen to the leaders of the trade-union, who acquaint the President of the nation—who to them is always "the beloved Colonel" of the Secretariat of

Labor and Welfare and also the "first Argentine worker"—with all the resolutions taken by the national assembly.

Afterward Perón is likely to speak to them at length on matters of national moment, informing them in this way how things are going.

This is very useful to everyone, because in this way each workers' delegation takes to a distant corner of the country a direct version of the words of the Leader. Frequently the General also speaks to the workers on subjects which can be dealt with only in direct and private conversation.

In this way the people know all that their guide thinks about all their problems, including those on which no one, except the President, could speak with a single word of authority.

With the exception of these numerous audiences, at which I assist only when the President invites me, I am not present during the calls paid by the trade-unions on the President on Wednesday afternoons.

And do not believe it is because I do not wish to be there.

But, as I have already said, my functions end where those of the President of the Republic begin.

There is still another reason. I want the workers always to speak to Perón alone, because not even I myself wish to seem at any time an obstacle between the people and their Leader.

The great misfortunes of many peoples and of many countries lie in the fact that the governors they have elected allow themselves to be "surrounded."

Whether well or badly surrounded, a governor who lets himself be surrounded establishes an obstacle between himself and his people!

If Perón has one wish and firm purpose, it is precisely that no one should interfere between him and his people.

That is why I myself am only a guide to him.

In this way I am something like a path by which the humble people, the working people, reach his presence.

And even I take much care not to be the only way, either, because that also would be a barrier between the people and Perón.

Once the workers are in the presence of the Leader, I retire, even when I remain in Government House, attending to other problems, which are never lacking among the trade-unions awaiting their turn for an audience.

Perhaps the secret of my success lies in many details such as these.

Details which have no apparent importance, which it is easy and profitable to attend to.

I would not be able to close this chapter without saying that Wednesday afternoons are generally happy afternoons for us.

At the end of the day we return home together, the Leader and I, to our private residence and I enjoy seeing him satisfied and happy; the contact with his *descamisados*, with the *grasas*[1]— as the selfsame workers are wont to call themselves—comforts him.

Very often at the end of one of these days he will say:

"We are getting on well. The 'boys' are contented!"

It makes me happy to see him satisfied, and it always moves me to think that a man like him, on the highest pedestal in the country, feels happy simply because of this . . . because a humble daylaborer, perhaps, has told him that *he is pleased with his President.*

---

[1]Affectionate term for *descamisados*, from *grasa*, meaning "grease."

93

25

The Great Days

BUT PERON'S HAPPINESS reaches its highest peak on the days when we celebrate our great anniversaries.

The 27th of November: Day of the Secretariat of Labor and Welfare. The 17th of October: Day of Loyalty.

The 1st of May: Labor Day.

On the two latter dates the people gather in extraordinary numbers, and on the very scene of our major glories, in the Plaza de Mayo.

The great public celebration is always organized by the General Confederation of Labor, and at it the workers of the capital and delegates from the interior of the country assist en masse.

I admit that the days before these greatest feasts of our movement are very busy ones for me.

Not because it is my business to have anything at all to do with their organizing, but because, as they are popular holidays, I take pains that all the workers are able to celebrate them with the greatest joy.

So I go over all outstanding problems of the various trade-unions, and to that end I receive their delegations, in an attempt to resolve these problems. In this way the gladness of the workers will be greater, and the holiday complete.

It would sadden me to see, from the balconies of Government

House on those solemn days, some organizations whose major problems had not, but could have, been settled.

It is not because I fear that some sector might be absent. No.

On the contrary, even under the most difficult circumstances for some syndicates, they have always been present to testify that the Leader is always a Leader to them—as they say, "in good times and bad."

On November the 27th we commemorate the day of the Secretariat of Labor and Welfare.

Though it is not a national holiday, since the whole country, including its public administration, works on that day as on all the other working days of the year, the workers do not forget to celebrate it worthily with a popular meeting held in front of the Secretariat building.

The date has an extraordinary significance. On that day, in 1943, the first year of the revolution, Perón converted the old and useless National Department of Labor into the Secretariat of Labor and Welfare.

I have already explained in these notes how that was the day the revolution really began.

For Perón, that day was one of triumph.

For the workers, it was the first day of sunshine after a long night of anguish and anxiety and of oligarchic exploitation.

The 1st of May, which in other years was a sad celebration by oppressed workers, is today one of our major festivals.

Sometimes visitors from abroad have asked us why the government perpetuates a date which today, all over the world, has come to have a revolutionary meaning, and which communists everywhere take advantage of to agitate against what these visitors call "legally constituted order."

I have always given the same answer to this, and I think that these jottings, intended to answer so many unasked questions, should contain the same replies which I have given to those who have questioned me personally.

In the first place, I do not think the government could "suppress" the celebration.

It belongs to the people!

And Perón has said many times that he will do nothing but what the people wish.

The people, who formerly suffered on each 1st of May the anguish of oppression, and even death, cannot do less than remember the date with gladness.

Before Perón, the workers on the 1st of May gathered in the public squares and in the streets of all the towns of the country, and their leaders took advantage of the opportunity to speak to them.

The good leaders, generally, had really very little to say; they could speak only of hopes—the realizations then were very few.

The bad leaders, the false leaders, those who had learned the lesson in foreign books or strange lands, did not lose the opportunity of inciting their companions.

In view of the few victories labor could offer, and of the long wait for promises that were never fulfilled, the easiest way was to excite the workers to rebellion and anarchy.

Governments, cold and inaccessible to all clamor and to all sufferings, responded to these events with silence or—more often than not—with the police.

And the 1st of May was almost always robed in red—because it was the day when humble blood was spilled—which is never blue, always red, because it is always pure!

The Argentine people does not forget those days of anguish and of death.

Why should it not celebrate the day, now that it can do so without fear and anxiety?

Instead of screaming with clenched fists in front of the closed doors of Government House, the Argentine working people now celebrate each 1st of May with a magnificent festival, at which their Leader presides from the balconies of Government House in his character of the "first Argentine worker," the title which, without any doubt, Perón appreciates most.

And the marvelous thing is that, instead of fearing death on that day, the people are wont to offer their lives, yelling a chorus which always moves my soul: "Our lives for Perón!"

The 17th of October is another thing.

But the people are the same, and the place, as always since 1945, is the Plaza de Mayo.

It is our "Day of Loyalty."

Since 1945, every year the *descamisados* of my country have held their tryst in that place.

As on that memorable first night, each year they want to see and hear Perón.

That is a day of great emotions for me.

Although I always intend to be strong to the end, I never quite manage it.

It is too much for my heart to contemplate at the same time the people's happiness and that of Perón.

From the balcony overlooking the celebration I am able to see the faces of the *descamisados* and the face of the Leader.

The spectacle is always magnificent, but it becomes indescribable when Perón speaks.

Every year he asks the people if they are satisfied with the government. When thousands and thousands of voices reply yes, the whole Plaza de Mayo shakes and I can affirm that this shaking, which springs from so many souls, shakes my heart violently.

What happens in the heart of Perón is perhaps very difficult for me to describe.

When I wished to portray in these notes the figure of the Leader, I said that it would be better to go out and see it, just as one might invite someone to see something indescribable, like the sun.

To say what is happening in Perón's heart each 17th of October is something like that.

I do not think that the explanation of the "magnetism" of the multitude on its Leader, and that of its Leader on the multitude, is true.

Instead, I believe it is more a matter of feeling.

I think that many men assembled together, instead of being thousands and thousands of separate souls, are, rather, only one soul.

For this soul to manifest itself, the Leader must have sufficient sensitiveness to hear the voices of the gigantic soul of the multitude.

That is why it is necessary to possess an extraordinary soul to be a leader.

And Perón's secret lies there: in his soul!

And that—his soul—is precisely what cannot be described, just as the sun cannot be described. It is not even possible to see it. One must comfort oneself with feeling its warmth, illuminating the way.

And that is what the people feel each 17th of October; that is what I feel in my infinite smallness, confronting each meeting of Perón with his people.

We feel the sun warming our skin and injecting its heat into our veins, giving us life.

We feel that the sun illuminates all our paths.

And when the day is ended we know that we have made one another happy.

The Leader has left his people contented and calm.

The people feel happy knowing that Perón continues to be the same as in 1945.

And Perón remains contented with his people.

The holiday ends when the people remember the strike on the 18th of October of 1945 and begin to shout:

"Tomorrow is St. Perón's Day!"

And then the Leader, as in 1945, resolves again this peaceful "strike" of a day, the only strike in the world that is not against anything or anyone, because, just as in 1945, the workers leave their daily tasks to celebrate the return of Perón.

That is why they cannot fail to celebrate the anniversary.

Generally on the night of October the 17th it is difficult for me to compose myself for sleep.

Because the affection of the people is a lovely dream, in the presence of whose incomparable beauty nothing better could be dreamed of.

And I like to prolong it in my memory, for in this way all the effort of living in this daily struggle is forgotten.

Eva Duarte Perón

And the necessary strength returns to continue the next day, like every day.

26

Wherever this Book is Read

WHEN I BEGAN to write these notes, I was guided only by the intention of explaining the motives, the causes and some of the aspects of the mission which has fallen to my lot in Perón's new Argentina. I wanted to explain why I took this path.

But at this stage of the work I think I have already paused many times—too often, perhaps—to describe somewhat the view bordering my path.

However, I am not sorry.

After all, why I live, how I live, and why I am what I am, is not likely to interest the world so much as an understanding of how a people live who believe themselves to be happy, and what they are like, and what the man is like who has been able to cause such great happiness!

Because, in reality, up to now, except for my first chapters, almost all the rest has been a description of the wonderful scenery along my path: Perón and his people!

And I say it here because I do not want to mislead anyone.

Perhaps tomorrow my only glory will consist of that: in having known how to tell all the truth regarding the great loves of my life, just as I live them, feel them and serve them!

For love is not understood or complete unless one serves it.

For me, love is service.

That is why all my life seems to me so easily explained.

The whole "secret" consists in this: I have decided to *serve* my people, my country and Perón.

And I *serve* because I love.

I serve the people because first the people won my heart. And because Perón taught me to know them better and consequently to love them better.

I serve Perón's cause and Perón himself however I can and whenever I can, always acknowledging that serving Perón is the same as serving the people. And I acknowledge it with gladness. May there not be in all this the "key," the explanation, of my own life?

I have already explained how I serve the workers.

Now I want to explain how I serve the humble.

But first, as a farewell gesture to the workers, two more words about them.

Two words of gratitude.

I desire that wherever this book is read, the feelings of my grateful heart should be known.

Because they were the first to have faith in Perón.

Because they believed even before seeing.

Because they never abandoned him.

Because they rescued him from his prison on October 17, 1945.

Because they made him President of the Argentines on February 24, 1946.

And, above all, I thank them for one thing: that they love him as they do!

And let this be known wheresoever this book is read!

27

Besides Justice

AMONG MY READERS, as in every corner of the earth, there are sure to be two classes of souls.

The class of narrow souls who cannot conceive of generosity, nor of love, nor of faith, nor even of hope, as realities.

If this book falls into the hands of a soul like that, I beg him not to continue further.

It is not worth while! It will all seem futile to him, or simply propaganda.

Here begin the chapters that none but those who still believe in sincerity, in faith, in love, and in hope will be able to understand.

These, indeed, I invite to continue a little further.

To them, as to the visitors of my works of social service, I shall go on showing, at the same time, how these qualities run through life, even through suffering.

I shall show them first the suffering of my people, and it will not be superfluous for us to stop and see it, as I have seen it, always larger and nearer, from the watchtower of my life.

I shall show them later what love does so that suffering smiles—and, smiling, lessens, or withdraws, or departs!

From the day I approached Perón I was aware that his

struggle for social justice would be long and difficult.

As he went on explaining his purposes to me (and his purposes were nothing less than changing an entire economic capitalistic system into one more worthy and more human, and thus more just), my forebodings were confirmed: the struggle would be long and difficult!

I saw a spectacle of many millions of Argentines awaiting justice; and at their head Perón, wishing to give to all that which was due to each.

And at the same time fighting against the forces conjured up by the unpatriotic and by powers foreign to the nation, determined to go on exploiting the good faith and the generosity of our people.

Although I believed in Perón, perhaps more than he himself believed in his own strength, I could never imagine that the greater part of his dreams—and what dreams they were— would be realized so quickly in my country.

His reasoning was simple. Perhaps too simple to convince ordinary men, who, as Perón is apt to say, "go in flocks like sparrows and fly low."

He used to tell me in 1945:

"Social justice demands a redistribution of all the riches of the country so that thus there may be fewer rich and fewer poor.

"But how can a government which has not the control of economic power redistribute the riches of the country?

"That is why it is needful for me to dedicate all my efforts to assuring the economic power of the country! Everything that is a means of economic dependence will have to be nationalized; and all that which forms an unnecessary expenditure of national riches. In this way there will be more riches for the people!

"In this way the people will have what they need, or at least all that belongs to them!

"All this, obviously, will take time . . . and many Argentineans will still die without being able to see the hour of justice!"

This last bit made me think that "meanwhile" it was necessary to do something else.

When Perón reached the presidency of the nation, it seemed to me that the moment to do that something else had arrived.

I knew, through Perón himself, that justice could not be done throughout the country from one day to another.

And, nevertheless, the Argentines, the *descamisados*, the humble, believed so much and so blindly in their Leader that they hoped for everything from him, and everything quickly, including those things which can be arranged only by a miracle—the scarcity of which is notorious in these times.

Undoubtedly, while Perón was willing to work with his life and soul in a justicialist undertaking, something more would have to be done.

I felt that that something more was up to me, but frankly I did not know how to set about it.

At last one day I took courage . . . I took courage . . . and launched an appeal of the heart!

"Here I am. I am the wife of the President. I want to be of some use to my people."

The *descamisados* who heard me passed the news on, one to another.

They began to come to me; some personally and others by letter.

In those letters they already began to call me "Evita."

Then I told them:

"I prefer being 'Evita' to being the wife of the President of the Republic, if that 'Evita' can be of any help to the *descamisados* of my country."

That is how my work of social service commenced.

I cannot say that it sprang from me.

Instead, it seems to me more exact to say that it sprang from a mutual and simultaneous understanding among my heart, that of Perón, and the great soul of our people.

It is a common task.

And that is what we feel it is: the task of all and for all.

28

The Sorrows of the Humble

I HAVE CARRIED over from the last chapter an invitation that I am extending in this one: like the visitors to my works of social service, I want to make my readers understand a little of the sorrow and the love of the people.

A little of the sorrow, first.

Here also, as all over the world, many years of social injustice have left painful memories of their past in every corner of the country.

When Perón raised the banner of social justice, among those who rallied to it the underdogs were infinitely more numerous than the few of the privileged classes who responded.

A few rich and many poor.

The wheat of our land, for example, served to satisfy the hunger of many of the privileged also in foreign lands; but the laborers who sowed and harvested that wheat here had no bread for their children.

The same thing happened with all other goods: meat, fruit, milk.

Our riches were an ancient lie to the children of this land.

A hundred years spent in this fashion had sown poverty and misery in Argentine towns and countryside.

I remember mentioning in one of my first chapters the scenes of misery surrounding our great capital when I was able to see it for the first time.

After five years of intense struggle in the government, and with all the efforts of the social service functioning intensely, the picture has not yet completely disappeared, although very little of it remains as a sad remembrance of the Argentina found by Perón.

For the day when even this memory shall have disappeared, I want to describe the scene a little—not from outside, like an artist, but from within, as I have seen it. As I have suffered, seeing it!

To see poverty and misery, it is not sufficient to draw near and gaze on it. Poverty and misery do not let themselves be seen so easily in all the magnitude of their suffering, because even in his saddest need a man, and even more a woman, knows how to manage to hide his own condition, at least a little.

That is why, when the rich approach those hives of low architecture, the poorer districts through which great cities usually spill themselves into the countryside, they do not see clearly.

Their subconscious minds are a little to blame for not letting them see the depths of reality.

And another reason is, as I have said, because poverty hides itself.

Unprepared visitors passing by will see huts of straw and mud, tin shanties, a few flowerpots and some plants; they will hear some more or less cheerful song; the chatter of children playing on the wasteland . . . and it might happen to occur to them to think that all this is poetic and perhaps romantic.

At least I have frequently heard it said that there are "picturesque" districts.

And to me this seemed the most sordid and perverse expression of the egoism of the rich.

"Picturesqueness" to them is men and women, old people and children, entire families, who have to live in homes worse than the sepulchers of any of the rich, even the moderately rich!

They never see, for example, what happens when night comes.

If there is a bed, there are not likely to be mattresses, or vice versa; or, there is simply one bed for everyone . . . and "everyone" is likely to be seven or eight or more persons, parents, children, grandparents . . .

The floors of the huts, shanties and slums are likely to be of bare earth.

The rain and the cold are apt to filter through the roofs. Not only the light of the stars, which would be the poetic and romantic thing.

Children are born, and with them a growing problem is added to the family.

The rich still believe that each child brings, according to the old proverb, a loaf of bread under his arm; and that where there is sufficient for three, there is also enough for four. It is easy to see that they have never witnessed poverty at close quarters!

And, in spite of all, there is happiness when none of the family is ill; though when this happens, then suffering reaches its bitterest extreme.

Then the parents' anguish, if the sick person is a child, for instance, knows no bounds.

I have seen them going through the streets, carrying the child in their arms, looking for a doctor, a drugstore, a hospital, anything; because not even the services of the *Asistencia Pública*[1] dare to enter those labyrinths of caves constituting the "picturesque" districts.

I have also seen them return home carrying the dead child, leave it there on a table and go out to find a coffin, just as previously they had gone out to find a doctor and medicine: desperately.

The rich are wont to say:

"They have no feelings. Don't you see they do not even cry when one of their children dies?"

And they do not realize that perhaps they, the rich, who have everything, have taken away from the poor even the right to cry.

No . . .! Evidently I will not be able to describe what life is like in any of these "picturesque" districts.

[1] Public First Aid Service.

And I resign myself to giving up the attempt.

But there is one thing I want to repeat here before proceeding further.

That the poor have no feelings is a lie started by the rich.

I have often heard from the lips of the "upper classes," as they are accustomed to call themselves, things like these:

"Do not worry so much about your *descamisados*. That kind of person does not have our sensitivity. They do not understand what happens to them. And perhaps it is better on the whole that they do not."

I can find no reasonable argument with which to refute this unjust lie.

I can do nothing but tell them:

"It's a lie. A lie you, the rich, invented yourselves, so as not to be troubled. But it's a lie."

If they asked me why, I would have only one thing to tell them, very little. It would be this:

"I have seen the humble cry, but not from pain, for even animals cry from pain! I have seen them cry out of gratefulness!"

And out of gratefulness, the rich, indeed, do not know how to cry.

29

The Beginnings

THE PICTURE I have vainly tried to describe was, at the beginning of the justicialist movement, a usual thing in all the cities of the country.

But the same also happened in towns and villages, and the smaller they were the worse it was.

And a similar thing happened in the countryside where tenants, colonists and laborers had suffered for many decades the effects of oligarchic oppression.

It is true that one of Perón's first measures of justice was to establish new conditions of wages and of work for rural laborers.

That was fundamental.

But before just wages and worthy working conditions could give their fruits of comfort, it was necessary to remedy also the grief of so many years.

Everywhere homes, clothes, health, were lacking.

That is why I had gone out into the streets to say:

"Here I am. I want to be of some use to my people."

When I noticed that my country's *descamisados* had listened to my then timid voice; when I began to see that letters arrived, and more letters, and men and women, youths and children and the elderly, began to knock on the doors of our private residence, only then did I realize what the "appeal from my heart"

111

would signify.

Although I had already foreseen that it was an almost impossible undertaking, I was convinced of it when the full meaning of the task became apparent to me.

Yet Perón had already taught me many things, and among them to delete the word *impossible* from my dictionary.

He, who flew "high and alone like the condors" (I use the words he is wont to apply to the men of genius he admires: San Martin, Alexander, Napoleon), had taken me out of the "flock of sparrows" and had given me my first lessons.

One, the first perhaps, was to make me forget the word *impossible*.

And we began. Bit by bit. I could not say exactly on what day. What I do know is that at first I attended to everything myself. Then I had to ask for help. And finally I was obliged to organize the work, which in a few weeks had become extraordinary.

It is true that from the first day I relied on the moral and material help of the President, but it was never a case of leaning too much on him who had other and much more serious problems than mine.

I remember at one time we were wondering whether it was expedient that I undertake the task, or whether perhaps it should be handled by some State organization.

And it was Perón himself who told me:

"Peoples much smitten by injustice have more confidence in persons than in institutions.

"In this, more than all the rest, I am frightened of the bureaucracy.

"In the government it is necessary to have much patience, and to know how to wait for everything to get going.

"But in works of social welfare it is not possible to wait for anyone."

This reasoning, logical and simple like all of Perón's, confirmed me in the post which he, the *descamisados* and I together had chosen for me.

30

Letters

EVERY DAY THE mail brings thousands of letters to our private residence.

All in humble envelopes.

In a simple yet eloquent manner the *descamisados* here—and also the *descamisados* elsewhere—are wont to send me their petitions.

Each one writes to me as best he can. Very seldom can it be noticed that the letter has been written by someone else . . . and then only because the interested party does not know how to write, or does not dare to do so, thinking, possibly, that if the letter is better written it will be more successful.

And in these cases very often the opposite happens, for not even the best literary style can take the place of the tremendous eloquence of one who needs clothes or a home or medicine or work or . . . any of the things which those who write to me need.

Mothers of families write me many letters.

At Christmas time and at Epiphany I receive an infinite number of letters from children.

Many elderly persons also are accustomed to send me their petitions.

A small portion of the correspondence lacks sense and contains strange petitions, impossible to satisfy.

113

But the immense majority know well what they want, and make their requests simply and reasonably in a few words, although always with marvelous eloquence.

The important thing to me is that these letters smack of the people, because, smacking of the people, they smack of truth!

One day Perón said wisely that he had been all over the country from one extreme to another, and, having seen all its beauties and marvels, at last he met its greatest and highest form of beauty: the people.

If anyone doubts the Peronista saying: "The best we have is the people," I would invite him to read my letters, just the letters that reach me in a single day from all the corners of the land.

After long experience I know now for certain that a letter is just as revealing as a face.

Naturally, in this kind of correspondence, it is very exceptional for anyone to try to deceive.

He who asks for a home or clothes or a sewing machine or work, or medicine or any of the things that a *descamisado* may ask for, is not likely to want to deceive us, because if what he asks for reaches him, when it arrives his lie would be discovered.

With the greatest pleasure I would allow my eternal critics to read the enormous quantity of heart-rending appeals which the letters of the humble consist of.

Only thus, perhaps, would they understand—if they still have a little intelligence and a little soul left—all the harm which a hundred years of oligarchic and capitalistic oppression has done to the country.

Only thus, perhaps, would they understand that social welfare is indispensible and urgent.

And perhaps, only thus would they forgive me—although I do not aspire to be forgiven—the words in which I have condemned them, each time it was necessary, for being there, as the causes—or at least as silent witnesses—of the oppressive exploitation that rules as law in the Arentina which Perón is curing of its old and painful wounds.

But indignation—always my old indignation—has caused

114

me to swerve a little from my subject.

All the mail that reaches me is classified immediately by about a hundred of my collaborators.

For this work I have chosen humble men and women.

It could not be otherwise. "Only the humble will save the humble," Perón always says.

And it is true. Just as the rich see in the suburban districts of huts and slums a picturesque landscape, so only the poor see more than outward appearances. A rich person would see only words . . . and, confronted by that enormous spectacle of pain and anguish, would not discern the faith and the love and the hope that each message brings to my hands. Perhaps nothing better to say would occur to them than:

"In all this, what a lot of lies they must tell her!"

And I write it because I have often felt that some of those who happened to gaze on my pile of daily correspondence have thought so.

At the most it probably struck them—and they have told me this aloud—that it would furnish abundant material for a psychological study.

And then they say that the poor do not possess "our" sensitivity.

This is what sometimes makes me burst into outbreaks of uncontrollable indignation: the rich, insensible to human sorrow, accusing precisely those who are suffering from the very fault of the overabundance of the rich, of having no feelings!

That is why men and women who have suffered much are those I have chosen to do the work for me which I cannot do personally: to read the letters that reach me, classify them and decide what can be done.

Once all is classified, I proceed every day to consider what can be settled promptly, and also that which, though at first sight it seems impossible to arrange, appears to be of great urgency to the pleader.

In special cases I suggest that those interested be summoned to an audience at the Secretariat of Labor and Welfare.

I will speak later about these audiences.

Obviously, among five, six and even at times ten and fifteen thousand letters which reach me in a day, many petitions remain in suspense.

Above all, when what is asked for is a home or work, the answer is not always one that can be given right away.

But often, even in these cases, when the writer has concluded that his letter has not reached me or that I have forgotten him, we give him the present he has asked for.

In general, I endeavor to settle each problem as soon as possible.

Only when it is impossible to settle it immediately does the letter get put aside until something can be done.

This system of letters must give results, because more arrive all the time. Also I cannot go anywhere· without men and women and children waiting for me with letters in their hands, to such an extent that when I go out I always have to allow for this and take a large handbag with me, or someone to act as postman!

We always quote one of Perón's sayings: "In the New Argentina, the only privileged are the children."

And I try to comply with this truth in my letters also.

Letters from the children always have a special priority.

I like to read them when I want to rest a little, or perhaps be comforted after some disappointment in other aspects of my struggle!

They are so innocent and so ingenuous.

As, for example, a little eight-year-old *descamisada* wrote to me, saying:

"*Dear Evita: For Epiphany I would like anything, as long as it is a keepsake from you. But I have no bicycle.*"

That is the whole letter. But who would refuse her a keepsake?

31

My Afternoons of Social Welfare

AUDIENCES WITH THE poor are a relaxation to me in the midst of many exhausting days.

Twice a week, at least, I devote the afternoon to this mission of acting as link between the humble and Perón; for though the *Fundación* settles most of these people's problems it would be nothing or would do nothing without Perón, the reason and the soul of my Social Welfare.

Well, Perón is the soul of all that I have done, of all that I do, and of all that I shall do that is good and right in my life!

And what I do in my audiences with the most humble *descamisados* of my people, the poor, is very simple.

I generally receive them at the Secretariat, although sometimes, when my time is short and there are many urgent questions to be discussed, I give them an audience at the Residence, too. But preferably I attend to them at the Secretariat, as a tribute to Perón who created it—and also—why should I hide it?—with the secret intention that the "house of the workers," as the Leader named it, should have a little more of the *descamisados'* affection each day.

In a room alongside my office, in the same spot where I

attend to the trade-unions, there pass in turn before my desk the families or persons who bring me their big or little problems.

There is a bit of everything in those "afternoons of social welfare": problems of housing, of evictions, of illness, of unemployment; but at the same time as these material problems, many bring me their intimate troubles, the strangest and the most difficult to arrange, because for them I have, often, nothing more than kind words and advice.

Men and women arrive, for instance, under the pretext of asking my material help, who just do not know what to do with their lives . . . I do not know why or for what reason they come to see me, nor what they expect me to give them. They are souls defeated by suffering and injustice. Hunger, persecution, misery have led them to fall into all kinds of error, and the moment comes when they do not know which way to turn.

These are the "secret" audiences.

For the majority of persons explain their problems to me aloud, but almost always in each audience there is a little that is "secret." Then they tell me things in a low voice, almost in my ear, and very often weeping.

Because of that, because I know the personal tragedies of the poor, of the victims of the rich and the powerful exploiters of the people . . . because of that, my speeches often contain venom and bitterness. Before the spectacle of a woman, for example, thrown out into the street by an arrogant and selfish oligarch who has deceived her with his idiotic words of "love," how small a thing it seems to me to shout with all my soul what I have so often shouted: that justice will be done inexorably, at all costs, whomever it may affect!

And hundreds of souls, destroyed, as in this case, by the selfishness of men, file past me each afternoon of social service.

I know some will never understand all this.

When they read these pages they will remark with smiling self-sufficiency that "this is too melodramatic."

I would like to shout at them:

"Yes! Of course it is melodramatic! Everything in the life of

118

the humble is melodramatic. The sorrow of the poor is not stage melodrama, vulgar melodrama, cheap and ridiculous to the average and selfish man. Because the poor do not invent suffering ...they endure it!'"

That is why I often shout till I am hoarse and lose my voice, when the growing indignation within me, almost like a wound in my heart, escapes during my speeches.

Often I have wished that my insults were blows or strokes of the whip so that, hitting many in the face, I could make them *see*—even if only for a moment—what I see every day in my audiences of social service.

And when I say that justice will be done inexorably, whatever it costs and whomever it may affect, I am sure that God will forgive me for insulting my listeners, because I have insulted them through love, through love of my people! But He will make them pay for all that the poor have suffered, down to the last drop of their blood!

Eva Perón prays at the Vatican. She interceded personally with police on behalf of communists who had demonstrated against her on her arrival in Rome

Crowds were Evita's stock-in-trade

Evita in action

Arriving in Milan on her 1947 European tour, the First Lady of Argentina and the world stops the show

32

Alms, Charity, Benevolence

PERHAPS BECAUSE MY deepest feeling is indignation in the face of injustice, I have managed to do my work of social service without lapsing into sentimentality or letting my feelings carry me away.

On the other hand, Perón has taught me that what I do for the humble of my country is nothing more than justice.

Some mediocre persons in the opposite camp have discussed, and I think must still be discussing—for I have no time to lose listening to them—my work. I do not care what they think of me or of what I do. It is enough for me to know that I do the best I can. But their discussions amuse me when they are not even agreed on a name to give the work I do.

No. It is not philanthropy, nor is it charity, nor is it alms, nor is it social solidarity, nor is it benevolence. It is not even social welfare, although to give it a more nearly appropriate name I have called it so.

To me it is strict justice. What made me most indignant when I commenced it was having it classified as "alms" or "benevolence."

For "alms," as far as I am concerned, was always a pleasure of the rich: the soulless pleasure of exciting the desires of the poor without ever satisfying them. And so that alms should be

121

even meaner and crueler, they invented "benevolence," and so added to the perverse pleasure of giving alms the pleasure of enjoying themselves happily with the pretext of the hunger of the poor. Alms and benevolence, to me, are an ostentation of riches, and power to humiliate the humble.

And very often, as well, at the height of hypocrisy, the rich and the powerful said that it was "charity," because they gave—so they thought—for the love of God.

I think that God must often be ashamed of what the poor receive in His name!

My work does not seek to be that kind of charity. I have never said, nor will I ever say, that I give anything in the name of God.

The only thing which can be given in the name of God is that which leaves the humble happy and contented; not what is given through an obligation, nor for pleasure, but what is given for love.

I do not know where I have read that love consists not only of loving others, but also of making oneself lovable. Well, that is what I wish my work to be.

So that nobody may feel himself less than he is by receiving the help I give him. So that all may depart contentedly without having to humiliate themselves by thanking me.

That is why I have invented an argument which has had happy results:

"If what I give you is not mine, why do you thank me for it?"

What I give belongs to those who receive it.

I do nothing but return to the poor what all the rest of us owe them, because we had taken it away from them unjustly.

I am nothing more than a means chosen by justice so that its ends may be accomplished inexorably.

That is why I work publicly. I do not pretend to do anything but justice, and justice should be administered publicly. I have said this so many times during my five years of struggle that today no one thinks it demeaning to come to my work-table.

That is why I never expect thanks, which are a form of humiliation, although the gratefulness of the humble moves me more than any other thing. Above all, because it is expressed so

122

sincerely.

I remember a letter from a woman to whom I had sent a sewing machine. She sent me five pesos from her first earnings. I am sorry not to have that letter by me so as to quote it here in its entirety, because there was nothing superfluous in it. In each line could be seen how pure and unsullied is the great soul of the poor. All the letters contain something of that greatness. An oligarch would say that the poor, too, know how to lie. I do not deny it, but I am sure that they tell far fewer lies than do the rich. And if they lie, after all it is through necessity, while the rich lie for pleasure.

All this seems to me to be turning into too much chatter.

No wonder sometimes General Perón says that I talk a lot!

But I am writing all these things as they spring from my heart. I am fearful of forgetting something which may make my readers understand what my mission is in Perón's New Argentina.

Not that I need to be understood.

No. But I would like my friends to understand Perón and his people . . . his *descamisados* . . . a bit more.

That is why I am making an effort to explain so much.

God grant that it serve some useful purpose. Then I shall be happy.

33

A Debt of Affection

ALL THESE THINGS the *descamisados* who come to me in their need have heard me say publicly, and everywhere.

That is why they come to me without feeling humiliated, and many of them cheer up in my presence.

I have wanted it to be so. And, even more, I have tried for it to happen so. That they should come to me, as if they asked for justice, as if they demanded a right.

In addition, they do not ask of me. What they ask for is that which has always been denied them and which Perón has promised them: a little comfort, a little happiness.

They thought it out well, really, coming here, to ask for the fulfillment of the word given by Perón. That is why I feel like just another of his employees, without any other salary but his affection and that of my people . . . nobody in the world earns as much as I do!

What is important is that Perón's word should be accomplished. Those who ask something of me, ask it of Perón; and asking Perón is not humiliating for anyone, not even for those of highest station. Still less for a *descamisado* who sees in him a father or a friend.

This is real, absolutely real.

When we go for our drives in the city or travel about the

country, I like to hear the cries with which people greet Perón.

They are *descamisado* greetings.

"Good-by, old man!" they cry.

"Good-by, Peroncito!"

"God grant you never die, Perón!"

"Good-by, Juancito!"

To the old oligarchic politicians, gentlemen with stiff collars and illustrious surnames, all this appears ridiculous and demagogic.

They never mixed with the people. Because it was repugnant to them to be with the people. Because they did not feel at ease among the "rabble."

And when some of them, more ambitious, mastered their repugnance and the inconvenience of attaining some position by using the people as a springboard, then the people treated them as persons of another class.

And if one of this type were not, for example, a doctor, they called him one so as to show him they did not feel at home with him.

With Perón the opposite happens. The people greet and treat him as though he were one of themselves, as though he were a member of the family.

And I am gladdened.

This is pure affection like no other kind on earth: disinterested and without measure: the pure affection of the people, which cannot be paid for except by works of love.

That is why, when I give any present, however small, I feel not only that I am paying a social debt, or a debt the nation owes its most humble sons. I feel I am paying a debt of love!

That is why I have so often said that I will go on striving, even to laying down my life, if it becomes necessary. Because a debt of affection such as I owe the people can never be paid in full except with one's life.

34

The End of the Day

ALMOST ALWAYS I am accompanied in my audiences of social service by foreign visitors, high government officials and friends of the Peronista movement. And I do not dislike it. On the contrary, I enjoy it.

The foreigners see personally that all the lies going about the world are untrue.

Functionaries and friends of the movement accompany me, and I like to see them also at my side. It is as well for them to see, from time to time, the clamor of the people and the grief of the people. In that way they will not turn oligarchs!

I have already stated that when things begin to go to the head of one of ours, he sometimes leaves off liking that contact with the masses—with the *descamisados*. And if he does not react quickly, he is lost.

I know that friends, functionaries and foreign visitors come to see my work because of me only and not because of the poor I attend to, and that often they come out of mere curiosity; nevertheless, I am much more grateful for one visit during my afternoons of social service than for a hundred at the Residence. Above all, this goes for the President's closest collaborators, for if there is one thing I fear it is that men of responsibility in the government, absorbed in their work, may lose contact with the

127

people, even against their own will.

Besides, the Ministers help me greatly in my tasks. And the more they visit me and see what I do, the more they help me.

Also I like the trade-union delegates who are having an audience with me to be present afterward on my afternoons of social service. As nearly all the money for my work comes from them, it is right that they should see how and on what it is spent. After all, I am nothing more than the administrator of goods held in common.

I always finish my work late on these days of social service, often after the subways, trains, and some of the streetcar lines have stopped running. Then the families I have attended to who live at a distance from the Secretariat would have serious difficulty in getting back to their homes if I could not count on the automobiles of my visitors.

What is amusing is that sometimes all the cars have gone, and then I have to use my own. More than once I have had to take a taxi to return to the Residence. Do not think that this is a great sacrifice for me. I love seeing the taxi-driver's surprise when he recognizes me. If he is a Peronista, he is very happy. And if he is not—well, I don't think this has ever happened to me—at least he would not be able to say that it is untrue that I work so late.

Generally, when I finish my work, I have supper with some of the friends who have been with me.

Sometimes we have supper at the Residence, sometimes at the *Hogar de la Empleada*.[1] During supper I often settle with my collaborators some problem which has been left over or has arisen during the day.

When the supper is at the *Hogar de la Empleada*, one of the works of the *Fundación*, I am always accompanied by a more numerous group of friends.

These suppers thus turn into something like a soiree; a Peronista soiree, naturally!

He who is a poet can "show off" there, just as can he who is a good speaker.

[1]Home for Women Employees.

128

The only condition is that no one must say a word which does not refer to our common Leader!

I bear in my heart pleasant memories of gatherings which lasted into the small hours and spontaneously converted themselves into warm and sincere tributes to Perón—who often, by that time, was already up, starting a new day!

Not infrequently when I arrived back at the Residence, Perón was ready to leave for Government House.

The General is likely to get a bit cross with me for these extremes in my unmethodical way of working.

But . . . I cannot help my nature. He is a military man and therefore the friend of order, and always works with method and discipline.

I could not do that even if I wished, perhaps because I am in the very van of the struggle, while he is in supreme command.

The worst of it is that often, so that the President may sleep peacefully, I have promised him to leave off work promptly and arrive home early.

He no longer believes these promises. He knows that when I have "social service" or "trade-unions" I shall not have supper with him, and that I shall go to bed when he is about to get up, or even later. When he gets angry, I am apt to tell him that, just as it would be dishonorable for him to arrive late anywhere, for me it would be a dishonor to finish my timetable punctually.

And, because of the tactful way I say it, he is becoming convinced that I am "a hopeless case"!

Some persons think my unmethodical way of working is intentional . . . for the purpose of propaganda or exhibition.

I would like my critics to devote themselves occasionally to this kind of "propaganda." The world would be a better place if there were more propaganda of this kind. I don't know whether I make myself clear.

What happens is very simple. I am besieged with petitions, and all are urgent. Those in need cannot wait. All want to see me. And I cannot attend to all of them.

Very often, however, when they see that I am tired, the

people waiting to see me go away until another day.

None who have gone away without seeing me can say they did not find me willing to receive them, for they have seen me work till I was tired.

If I did not do this, many would remain discontented, thinking I did not want to see them . . . As it is, all know that I have neither time nor strength enough for all of them to go away satisfied, which is what I want.

35

Friends in Misfortune

I WANT THE Secretariat always to be something like home to all the Peronistas of my country.

There the name of Perón was born for all *descamisados*.

There he taught us the road to happiness and greatness. There we knew the magnificent and extraordinary nobility of his soul.

That is why I like the men and women who form the bloc of the Peronista movement to come to the Secretariat, even when Perón himself is not there.

I always greet them with affection; and even if it is not always possible for me to attend to them for very long, they know that when they need me they will always find me there—that is to say, they will find Perón, because I never wish to be anything more than his shadow in his old Secretariat ... that of the Leader and guide of the Argentines!

The Peronista movement, like all big revolutions, did not come about without sacrificing a few of the men who carried it out.

If someone did not bother to look after these men who remained by the wayside, they would form a nucleus, resentful and bitter, and would be at least a slur on a movement which wants to include all the people in its love and justice.

Sometimes they are men who have committed serious faults, or those who have taken roads too difficult for their strength; or vanity has turned their heads and giddiness caused them to fall from the heights; or some other reason has caused them to be eliminated from leading positions in the movement, and they have had to descend again to the plains.

This frequently happens in our struggles, because Perón covers the stages of each march with extraordinary impetus . . . so extraordinary that many persons fall behind and have to be replaced by fresh forces.

This same accelerated advance of Perón's does not allow him to stop to console the fallen and displaced.

At other times it is a matter of men who fall unjustly in the small struggles which are never lacking in the sectors of the party itself.

I receive all of them in my office.

They are neither workingmen nor poor, and they have nothing to do with the woman's movement . . . but they are Peronistas in misfortune, and that is sufficient for me!

And I always remember one of my favorite Peronista sayings: "To a Peronista there is nothing better than another Peronista."

I would say: "To a Peronista there is nothing better than another Peronista, and with still more reason if he is in disgrace."

Very often I have received Peronista friends whom nobody would receive: neither Ministers, nor leaders of the party. And these Ministers and leaders were right in refusing an audience.

At first I had to stand some bitter criticism.

I remember, for example, the case of a Minister who had to remove a high official from office, and who reprimanded me because a few hours afterward I received him cordially in my office.

Those impulses of the heart cost me a few headaches, but I explained myself as best I could.

I remember that I explained it to Perón, more or less like this:

132

"It is a matter of men of the movement whom we cannot leave lying about the side of the road. If, in spite of the failure and error they are punished for, they remain Peronistas at heart, that is sufficient merit for those who have never suffered any defeat."

The General approved of my reasoning.

That is why I continue attending to fallen and displaced Peronistas, and Peronistas in disgrace.

And very often I have found in them aptitude for something else, and have steered them along some other path, and they have triumphed.

I have remembered this strange mission of mine in the midst of these chapters devoted to social service, because if this job of attending to friends in misfortune is not social service, it has, nevertheless, the same sense of justice and of affection.

The others, those who have never tasted defeat, never been in difficulties, never failed in spite of good intentions, cannot imagine how hard these moments can be.

All the world keeps its distance from one who has fallen.

All the world wishes to forget him. Men ought to be kinder about this. All of them. We too, the Peronistas.

We forget the Peronista saying:

"To a Peronista there is nothing better than another Peronista."

I have already said it before, but it is necessary to repeat it very often until nobody forgets it and all follow it aright.

In this also we should be different to the oligarchy.

They become rich and powerful by dint of destroying the others, by dint of others' disgrace.

We must not be like them.

That is why I take care to attend to fallen friends.

So as not to feel I have the soul of an oligarch: selfish, sordid, incapable of any generosity.

After this explanation, I feel sure that those who sometimes did not understand my "impulses of the heart" will understand me a bit better.

Furthermore, in case any doubt remains, I venture to ask

them to remember just one thing. In every fallen Peronista I feel the desolation of that October of 1945 . . . when all doors were shut to me. And all hearts!

36
My Greatest Glory

THESE NOTES ARE actually turning out like any of my days, in which everything is muddled up: trade-union audiences or those of social welfare, official events, diplomatic visits, politics, attention to works in progress . . . and goodness knows how many other things from I can't tell how many pigeon-holes.

For each thing accomplished brings another in its train, and there is nothing to be done about it except to go ahead. I already regret that life, however long it may be, is so short, because there is too much to do in such a short time.

But it is better this way. Goodness knows how boring it would be to live if there were time to spare!

My audiences of social service, for instance, have obliged me to start other enterprises in my life.

As soon as I began to attend to the poor I realized that it was not only a matter of attending to them. More important than attending to them was to get results.

They ask. And they ask because we have told them that they have the right to those things which a miserable century of exploitation and injustice denied them.

Therefore we are under the obligation to give them what they have the right to ask for.

That is why I had to organize my help.

To give them clothes, utensils, beds, coverlets, sewing machines, building material, etc., I had to create large deposits which are now my greatest pride.

To give them homes I had to build these homes, and to build them I had to organize teams of technicians and workingmen and then set them to work all over the country.

To attend to the pressing need for shelter so often felt by the poor through extraneous and unforeseen circumstances, and until more permanent arrangements can be made, I had to build "temporary homes" in which to lodge women and children belonging to families in misfortune.

To attend to destitute old people, I had to build homes for the aged.

Requests for children's toys made me think that it was better for the gifts to arrive on an appropriate day, and so every year for Epiphany the *Fundación* does its duty to the children, who are, in Perón's New Argentina, "the only privileged ones."

The same thing happened with the cider and *pan dulce*,[1] which reaches all the humble homes in my nation at Christmastime, chiefly as a symbol of Perón's love for his people.

To be able to shelter orphaned or abandoned children, the construction of the home-schools had to be organized all over the country, because misery had claimed its victims everywhere among the children.

Thus, little by little, all that is now a reality came into being; and it went on growing, almost by force of circumstances.

All had its original cause in that "patriotic impulse" of mine when I went out into the street offering "Evita's" heart to my people.

And I do not regret it!

The work is great, but it is full of small and big joys. Sometimes in my enthusiasm to build, with the fever to accomplish great things which I have caught from Perón, my plans become complicated . . . and great difficulties appear.

Now, to tell the truth, difficulties worry me less than they do my collaborators. I have accustomed myself to find a solution to

[1]A spiced loaf.

most seemingly insoluble problems, and none of them worries me overmuch.

God is more the God of the poor than of the rich . . . and also—as Perón is apt to say—God has to be helped, so that He may help us.

And I think that at the *Fundación* we help Him plenty!

The work given by these undertakings is compensated by the joy of inaugurating them, of seeing them serve the humble, the children, old people, the *descamisados* made a little happier.

I never enjoy the fruit of my labors so much as when the General visits my works. Very often we visit the children's town together, the temporary homes, the homes for the aged and for children, the Home for Women Employees, the residential districts.

I feel very happy to see the joy on Perón's face during these visits, which rest and refresh him among so many efforts and so many struggles on his path.

And his words of encouragement and gratitude are my best reward.

He often says to me:

"The Government could not do any of this. The State has no 'soul,' it has no spirituality. And this cannot be done without love."

And though many think that I must have grown accustomed to praises from the General, certainly no decoration, no prize, seems better to me than his words.

When we inaugurate our works Perón is always present at the ceremony we arrange for each. Naturally, he is the guest of honor.

This kind of ceremony is very simple.

I say a few words first, offering him the building.

Then the workingmen who built it, often at great sacrifice and always with much love, offer him their work.

And then Perón thanks us.

Very often when I finish my short address he rewards me with a kiss on the forehead.

No one can imagine what his proof of gratitude means to me.

Eva Duarte Perón

No glory in the world could ever be greater or purer than the glory in my heart on these joyful days.

37

Our Works

MAY I GO ON speaking a bit more about our works?

At this juncture I realize that sometimes I have written *my* works, while at others, such as now, I call them *our* works.

But either form is correct.

They are *mine* to a certain extent; and to a certain extent they are *ours*.

They are mine because I put all my heart into them.

Engineers and architects of the *Fundación* design large-scale plans . . . but afterward I put into each undertaking all that they have not perceived.

Above all, it was difficult for me to get them to understand that the *Fundación* homes were not asylums . . . that hospitals should not be anterooms to death, but anterooms to life . . . that dwelling places should not be just places in which to sleep, but places in which to live happily.

It was not their fault that at first they did not understand me.

For a hundred years the narrow soul of the rich could think of no better way to silence the voice of conscience than to dole out crumbs of charity to the poor.

Charity meant not only the cold and miserable coins the rich dropped into the outstretched hands of the poor. Charity was also the few asylums that they built with what was left over from some heritage of many millions.

All "social service" of the century which preceded us was like that: cold, sordid, mean and selfish.

In every asylum built by the oligarchy, there is evidenced the exploiting soul of a breed which, happily, will die out in this century, a victim of its own pride, its own selfishness.

The children "they" tried to "save" will never forget that "they" were their offshoots.

"They" made them communists by putting them in drab uniforms, giving them insufficient meals, shutting all doors to human happiness—to the simple happiness of having a home, or at least an imitation of a home.

They fertilized the soil for communism when to the poor of the world they applied the contemptuous term *rabble*.

Now they have realized their mistake. But it is too late.

With or without bloodshed, the race of oligarchic exploiters of mankind will die out, without any doubt, in this century.

And the ideas they created in the narrowness of their innermost souls (if they had any souls!) will die also.

The honor of destroying these old ideas has fallen to me through my work.

That is why my homes are generously rich. But here, I even want to surpass myself. I want them to be luxurious. Precisely because a century of miserable asylums cannot be wiped out except by another century of "excessively luxurious" homes.

Yes, excessively luxurious. I do not care if some "duty callers" flutter their skirts while they politely say to me:

"Why so much luxury?"

Or ask me, almost ingenuously:

"Aren't you afraid they will get accustomed to living like the rich?"

No, I am not afraid. On the contrary, I wish them to accustom themselves to live like the rich ... to feel worthy to live amid the greatest riches. For when all's said and done, everyone has a right to be rich on this Argentine soil ... and in any part of the world.

The world has sufficient available riches for all men to be

rich.

When justice is done, no one will be poor, at least no one who does not want to be.

That is why I am a justicialist.

That is why I am not afraid for the children in my homes to become accustomed to live like the rich, as long as they keep the souls they brought with them: souls of the poor, humble and unsoiled, simple and happy.

What makes my works my own is that they set a seal of indignation against the injustices of a bitter century for the poor.

That is why they say I am "socially resentful."

And my critics are right. I *am* "socially resentful." But my resentment is not what they think it is.

They think resentment is reached only along the path of hatred. . . . I have arrived at the same destination along the path of love.

And this is not a play on words.

On the contrary! Until I reached the place I hold in the Peronista movement, I was only indebted to it for its "civilities." Even a representative group of oligarchic ladies invited me to join their high circle.

My "social resentment" does not spring from any hatred. Only from love: from the love of my people, whose suffering has opened forever the doors of my heart.

But in everything else the works of the *Fundación* are "ours." And in calling them ours, I am nearer to the truth than in calling them mine.

Because the inspiration and courage was given to me, and still is given, by the gigantic soul of Perón.

Because the people, all the working people of my country, help me with their moral and material support in everything constructed by the *Fundación*.

And because, as Argentines, we all have the right to enjoy their benefits.

My ambition, for instance, would be to pass the last days of my life in any of my "Homes for the Aged," and each time I visit them I am glad to think I would feel comfortable and happy in them.

Very often the General has said the same to me.

It is the highest praise I have heard said of my works!

38

Christmas Eve and Christmas

TODAY IS CHRISTMAS, Christmas of 1950.

Last night, in five million Argentine homes, toasts were drunk in the cider, and the spiced loaves from "Perón and Evita" were eaten.

This, too, our adversaries have severely criticized.

They have told us that we throw crumbs onto the tables of the Argentines so as to buy the good will of the people.

We go on doing the same thing in the same way every year.

"Do they bark? It is a sign that we are on the move!"

But they are not crumbs. I know that instead of one bottle of cider, a dozen of champagne would be better . . . and instead of one spiced loaf, a hamperful of gifts.

But the average person does not realize that our cider, and our spiced loaves, are nothing more than a symbol of our union with the people.

It is our hearts (mine and Perón's) that wish to be united on Christmas Eve with all the hearts of the country's *descamisados* in an immense, fraternal, affectionate embrace.

In some way or other, we want to be with those at table in Argentine homes.

We have chosen this way because it seems to us the most friendly and the most appropriate.

A present, however costly, sometimes offends.

But the simpler a token or remembrance, the more love it seems to carry with it.

This is what we wish to send to each Argentine home with our cider and spiced loaves.

Last night, as I do every year on Christmas Eve, I addressed the *descamisados* in a radio broadcast.

Christmas Eve belongs to the poor, the humble, to the *descamisados*, since Christ, despised by the rich who shut all their doors against Him, was born in a stable. And didn't the angels appear to the shepherds, the poorest and most humble men of Bethlehem, and to them only tell the good tidings of Him who had come to bring happiness to the world?

Only to the shepherds, to the humble, to the poor, was the message given of "peace on earth to men of good will . . ."

What is there unusual in Perón's fighting only for the happiness of the *descamisados*?

The others, the oligarchs, already possess the happiness they have been able to build up for themselves.

This subject and the day make me continue to speak about God and the poor.

Often, when I think of my destiny in the mission I have to carry out, in the struggle which that mission demands of me, I feel weak.

The struggle is so great, and my strength so little!

In those moments, I think I feel the need of God.

I do not invoke the help of God at each moment.

I remember that one day someone begged me to be more "Christian," and to call more frequently on God in my speeches and in my public activities.

I want to state here in these notes the reply I gave, because I have promised to be sincere in everything.

"What you say is right. I do not call on God very often. The thing is, I do not want to mix God up with the muddle 'of my things.' Also, I hardly ever worry God by asking Him to remember me, and never ask anything for myself. But my love of Christ is much greater than you would think: I love Him in the *descamisados*."

For did He not say He would be in the poor, the sick, in those that hungered and those that thirsted?

I do not think that God requires us always to have His name on our lips. Perón has taught me that it is better to have Him in the heart. I am a Christian and a Catholic, and I practice my religion as best I can, and firmly believe that the first commandment is that of love. Christ Himself said: "Greater love hath no man than this, that a man lay down his life for his friends."

If I ever trouble God with any petition of mine it is for that: for Him to help me to give my life for my *descamisados*.

39

My Work and Politics

WHEN I ENVISAGED my work of social welfare, I did not even re-
motely dream that I should have to do all that I was afterward
obliged to do.

The necessities of the poor compelled me.

It is this which makes my work different from that carried out
by decadent societies of "benevolent ladies."

They built because of their own need. They had to salve their
own consciences, whose dregs of Christianity reminded them
occasionally that the gates of Heaven are very narrow for all the
rich. As narrow as the eye of a needle!

On the other hand, the works of the *Fundación* sprang from
the needs of the *descamisados* of my country.

Work of social welfare built by the "ladies" in the old Argentina were planned by persons who always ignored the needs of
the poor.

In the New Argentina our works spring from an increasingly
deep knowledge of these needs.

Added to which, the money for our works comes from the
people themselves. It is not superfluous money from anyone's
pocket; often it is money which reaches my hands thanks to the
sacrifices of many workers together.

The other was superfluous money, perhaps stolen money—

for any money left over in the pocket is, in a certain sense, money belonging to someone else.

The money for my works is sacred, because it is the very *descamisados* themselves who give it to me, to be distributed as fairly as possible.

That is why Perón says it is "a miracle unique in the world."

I think this miracle is possible only when a people is as generous as the Argentine workers.

That is why the works of the *Fundación* are distributed all over the country. A home-school for children is of no use to anyone if the work is not completed by a chain of homes such as are being built in all Argentine provinces and territories.

The same goes for homes for the aged, for hospitals.

Neither can works of social service have political leanings.

I do not deny that my work helps to consolidate the enormous political prestige enjoyed by the General, but never have I subordinated love to self-interest . . . and still less when it is a matter of the love of my people.

And I have thousands of proofs of this. Many of my works are erected in almost desolate spots where there are no votes to win.

What political interest can there be in building a Home in Tierra del Fuego?

Also, Perón no longer needs more votes. The only thing I can look for in my works is that the people's votes for Perón should have one more motive—that of gratefulness!

And, obviously, if I can manage to bring this about, I shall not leave off my efforts.

40

The European Lesson

WHEN I DECIDED to visit Europe I had one wish: to see what Europe had accomplished in the way of social welfare.

I had not yet begun to build, except in a timid fashion. I wanted to learn from the experiences of the older nations of the world.

Every time I got the chance, secretly or publicly, I visited European social welfare undertakings. Today, three years after that journey (an account of which I shall leave for another occasion), I can say that, save for a few exceptions, I learned from those visits of apprenticeship all that a work of social welfare in our country should *not* be. The peoples and governments I visited will forgive me, I trust, for this very outspoken but very honest statement.

On the other hand, they—peoples and governments—are not to blame. The century of capital's exploitation of the workers left its mark on the Old World, too.

Our only advantage is that we have not had the misfortune of suffering the added horror of disastrous wars, and instead have been privileged to be given by God a guide of Perón's caliber.

Here, we are in full daylight; there, night is only beginning to disappear.

The immense majority of the social service works of Europe

are cold and poor. Many have been built according to the standards of the rich . . . and when the rich think of the poor, they think poorly. Others have been erected by State standards; and the State can only build bureaucratically, that is to say, with coldness, from which love is lacking.

I came back from Europe thinking that Christianity had already passed over her, leaving behind everywhere great and beautiful memories. But only memories!

And on the ship which brought me back I often thought of Perón's ideals; above all, of that first principle of his doctrine, which says: "Our doctrine is profoundly Christian and humanist."

Even from on board I wrote the General some of my thoughts, from which I will quote a few paragraphs:

"Our doctrine must be Christian and humanist; but in a new way; in a way which I think the world has not yet known. The Christianity of our movement, such as you dream of realizing, is not what I have seen in the countries of Europe which I visited.

"I will help you with my works. Already I am depending on your help . . ."

Further on I said:

"In Europe all seems to be history; we in Argentina see everything as though it were about to happen. Europeans, on the other hand, no longer look forward, but backward.

"While they were telling me, for example: 'Look at this tenth century cathedral,' I thought of the home-schools I will start as soon as I arrive in Buenos Aires. When they were showing me an ancient historic volume, I thought that *we* are already at the beginning of another volume, in our country . . . and with your name."

Three years after those letters were written, I cannot but admire myself, seeing how what I dreamed of then has come to pass.

Above all, in the works constructed do I see clearly that I learned the lesson of Europe well.

In each of them I have tried to make the humanistic Christianity in Perón's doctrine evident to those who come after us.

That is why each home, be it "temporary," for children, or for the aged, is built as though it were for the richest and most exacting of men.

Can that ingenuous idea of my childhood, when I thought everyone in the world was rich, still be noticed here, by any chance?

I think it is inhuman to add another misery, however small it be, to the misery of those who suffer. That is why my hospitals are meant to be happy: their walls artistically decorated, with no white beds, their windows large and their curtains homelike . . . so that no patient may feel he is in a hospital!

When an undertaking is planned and built, I always plan the bedrooms as if I were planning my own.

Who can say for certain that I will never have to stay in a temporary home, or one for the aged, or in a hospital?

If the place satisfies me, then I am happy, knowing that nobody in it will ever feel humiliated, or that his dignity has been offended.

While I wrote these lines I asked General Perón:

"Have I kept the promise I made you when I returned from Europe, when I offered to help you so that the Christianity of your doctrine should be carried out in works of social welfare?"

His reply was more than generous:

"Without your help I could have done nothing. You have taught us to build with love!"

To me this is not a reward, but glory itself.

41

The Measure of My Works

PERHAPS I CANNOT successfully describe the outward forms of the works of the *Fundación*, their architecture, or the internal arrangement of the sections, or even the way in which they work.

But I would like to refer to details which make evident the spirit I have tried to instill in them.

They are details of perhaps no apparent importance.

In my "homes," no *descamisado* should feel that he is poor.

That is why there are no degrading uniforms. Everything must be homelike, friendly, cheerful: the corridors, the dining rooms, the bedrooms.

I have banished the long tables, the cold, bare walls, the beggarly dinner service. All these things are of the same style and the same quality as in the home of a well-to-do family.

The tables in the dining room have bright, colorful cloths, and flowers must not be lacking, as they never are in any home where there is a mother or a wife who is more or less fond of her family.

The walls, too, must be friendly and bright, with pleasing and interesting pictures, suitably framed.

Suitable crockery and cutlery.

As a result, my *descamisados* may say when I visit them in my homes what so often I have heard them say:

"Evita, I feel better here than at home."

The children in my homes do not wear any kind of uniform.

Each of them has clothes of the color he likes. The only stipulation is that he must choose something good; because these children are accustomed to poverty, they must not choose the worst!—although this very seldom happens . . . good taste is the last thing lost through poverty!

I have not wished the children in the homes to be cut off from the rest of the world. That is why they go to official schools, like all the rest, and mingle with children who have parents and homes, so that no one can tell the difference between them. (If they are not easily noticed by being better clothed and fed than the others!)

In the home-schools the children live in the greatest possible freedom (and even more so do the aged in their respective homes).

They may have a little money, and if they have none we give them some so that they may feel freer.

We cultivate the natural bent of each child, especially when it is in the field of an art or trade.

In a word, everything is more "home" than "school."

The bedrooms are the largest possible, so that the inmates shall not feel as though they were in a barracks.

And in all the rooms of the house, bright and pleasing curtains contribute to cheerfulness.

Many other details must be omitted because it would take too long to mention them.

The best thing would be for those who can do so to go and see for themselves.

All is open to the eyes of friends. And even to those who do not understand!

It is better to go and see. I know that even thus there will be some who do not understand. But those who see with clear eyes, without personal prejudice, will not go away without thinking that the social service we accomplish is genuine, well intentioned, and perhaps blazes a new trail in the generosity of man.

Naturally, all my work is not made to the measure of the average man, whose mediocrity dims his vision.

It is impossible to forget that I have always tried to think and to feel as Perón thinks and feels.

And his soul is too big to be understood by the mediocre.

A little of the great marvel of his soul has undoubtedly remained in my work, and can be appreciated only when approached with generosity and not with mediocre selfishness.

Those who see my works should not forget that they have been built according to the measure of my love for Perón and for his people . . . which is a love without measure!

42

A Week of Bitterness

THE ROLE OF "Evita" is also bitter at times. All this past week, for instance, I have found it bitter.

There has been a strike, and it had to be declared unjust and illegal.

I know that bad leaders—the old leaders of anarchical syndicalism and of socialism, and infiltrated communists—have directed all this.

I know that the greater part of the trade-unions and that all the people have repudiated the actions of these ungrateful ones, unworthy to live in this New Argentina of Perón's.

I know all this, and yet all during the week life to me has been bitter. I felt better only when I decided to go out and see the workshops and talk to the strikers themselves.

I was accompanied by two workingmen from the General Confederation of Labor.

I wanted to go without a guard or escort, which I never use, and for whom there was no reason on this occasion, when I was going to see what was happening to the workingmen on strike.

So I went as a friend, and as a friend I could not go to them as though I were afraid, or were even taking precautions.

Added to which, I think fear has left me forever.

I spoke to the workingmen in each place. Of course they

157

never expected to see me turn up, especially at the hour I did; the expedition took from midnight until four-thirty in the morning. In this way I could verify that the strike was ill-advised and unjust, since even the workers themselves did not know the reasons for the stoppage.

In this way I was able to inform the President of the entire truth, the truth of the man in the street, which to a governor is fundamental if he wants to call himself democratic, that is to say, the governor of "a government of the people, by the people."

I will not deny that my emotion was very great on meeting loyal and unselfish men in each workshop who were willing to do anything rather than what they felt was treason against the one and undisputed Leader of the mass of Argentine workers.

But that emotion could not wipe out the bitterness from my soul.

For I cannot conceive how there can be a single workingman in my country who has not yet understood what Perón is and all that Perón has done for the Argentine workers.

Although the strikers may be few, it hurts me as much as though it were all of them.

I cannot understand it!

That is why I went out the day before yesterday!

I wanted to know if the workers knew what they were doing.

But when I realized that they did not, it did not make me any happier either; I thought there was still much to be done before the Argentine working masses could have full understanding of the responsibility of their historic mission, which is nothing less than to teach the world how to live happily in the shelter of Perón's justicialism.

This chapter is not a reproach.

If this book were intended as propaganda, perhaps I should not have written these somewhat sad pages.

But we—Perón always says—will win through the truth.

We will never say that we live without problems and worries. That would be a lie, and no one would believe us.

No. We have problems. We have worries. We also have our

sorrows.

But each time we get through them more united, and each time a little happier; because our people do not fail to follow us with loyalty and affection. On the other hand, each problem solved by Perón, energetically, without violence, and always consulting the people in some way, brings us closer to all the Argentines.

Some day the enemies of justicialism will be convinced that they can do nothing against the truth, because truth always asserts itself—above all when he who defends it has Perón's extraordinary qualities of intelligence and heart.

This chapter may seem out of place in the midst of these jottings intended to explain my mission.

But those who wish to see clearly the entire picture of life itself should see not only the highlights. It is useful for them also to know the sorrows.

To know that my mission in this world stricken by war, hatred, anguish and desperation, though a mission of love and of justice, has to have its bitter hours.

Precisely because of that!

43

A Drop of Love

I KNOW MY social welfare work is not a definite way of settling any problem.

The only solution would be social justice. When everyone has that which justly belongs to him, social welfare will not be necessary. My greatest ambition is that someday nobody will need me. I should feel happy, immensely happy, if so many appeals for help stopped coming to me, because they show that the injustice which a century of bitterness brought the dispossessed is still reigning in some corner of my country.

I do not forget, however, that Perón told me one day:

"Justice cannot complete its work all at once. Perhaps it will take many years."

Yes. I know there is still a lot of suffering of which I have not even been able to hear. The appeals for help that reach me are limitless, and I know I shall not always be able to come to the rescue. To the thousands of letters written me by the *descamisados* of my own country, thousands and thousands are now added every day in the appeals I receive from the *descamisados* of the whole world.

It is impossible for me to cope with it all, however much money or however good the organization I have.

But, I resign myself to showing my good intentions to all. I know that my work is like a drop of water in the ocean. Or rather: it is a drop of love falling on that immense muddy ocean which is the world of hatred and strife.

But it is a drop of love. I know the world needs a rain of justice. That is why one day it will embrace Perón's justicialism, and be happy.

Meanwhile I am resigned to being simply that: a drop of love.

Sometimes I get a bit mixed up. I say that my work of social service is only justice, and then I feel that in reality it is a work of love.

And in both cases I am right.

Yes. It is justice, because I can never manage to give more than what rightfully belongs to the *descamisados*. I am only repaying what was taken from them during a century of treachery and of oligarchic privilege.

And it is also love, because my heart is in my work—the poor heart of a humble woman who does indeed do it for love.

For love of Perón.

For love of the *descamisados* of her people—and, why should I not say so?—of all the *descamisados* of the world.

44

How Perón and the People
Pay Me

BUT THE LOVE in my work does not wish to be sentimentalism, which I always consider ridiculous and stupid.

I never forget that my task is one of strict justice. I go to work each day as though it were just any kind of job, as though I were paid to do what I do.

I have no salary. I am not a government functionary under any aspect. I am free, absolutely free.

That is how I have wished it. Very often the General himself has wished to add me to his government as official collaborator.

I want to continue to be free and I think it is best; for him, for everyone else, and for me as well.

If I became a functionary I should stop being part of the "people." I could not be what I am, or do what I do.

Also, I have always been disorderly in my way of doing things; I like disorder as though it were my normal way of life. I think I was born for the revolution. I have always lived at liberty. Like the birds, I have always liked the fresh air of the woods. I was not even able to tolerate that degree of servitude which is part of life in one's parents' home or the life of one's home town. Very early in life I left my home and my town and

163

since then I have always been free. I have wished to live on my own, and I have lived on my own.

That is why I could never be a functionary, which means being tied to a system, chained to the great machine of State and fulfilling a definite function there every day.

No. I want to continue to be a bird, free in an immense forest.

I enjoy liberty as the people enjoy it, and in that, more than anything else, I recognize that I am completely of the people.

Although I am not a government functionary and receive no salary, still I go to work exactly as though I were, as though I were being paid for it.

And in reality I am paid, not in money but in other things with more than money—and how I am paid!

The people pay me with their affection.

I have said that my work is really the payment of a debt. I shall never forget the 17th of October, 1945.

That day I was paid in advance for all this that I am doing now.

Last night, a woman among my *descamisados* was crying, thanking me for something or other.

She told me that on October 17, 1945, she had been in the Plaza de Mayo.

That poor woman will never know the desire I had to do to her just what she did to me: to kneel down and thank her with my tears, kissing her hands.

How I have been repaid!

Perón also repays me with his affection and his confidence.

I know that because of my work I often cause him some disappointment.

Because I get home late—almost when he is getting up.

Because he thinks my disorderly way of working will make me ill.

Because I spend so little time with him.

Because sometimes, thinking to be useful to him, I do something unusual that turns out to be wrong. But he always forgives me.

He has been able to reconcile "slavery" and liberty in me.

As a woman I belong to him utterly, I am in a manner of speaking his "slave"; but never have I felt as free as I do now.

I would not take one step if I did not think it was in accordance with his wishes; and yet I feel as free as I have ever wished to be. I certainly do not know the explanation of this strange mystery, but I think that the unusual greatness of his soul must have something to do with it.

One day I read a book by Leon Bloy about Napoleon, in which the writer said that he could not imagine Heaven without his Emperor.

I liked this, and in a speech said that neither could I imagine Heaven without Perón.

Some thought that was almost heresy.

Yet, every time I remember it, it seems to me more logical.

I know that God Himself fills the heavens.

But God, Who could not imagine Heaven without the Mother He loved so much, will forgive me if my heart cannot imagine it without Perón.

45

My Gratitude

I KNOW THAT many details, and even many larger aspects of my work of social service, cannot be made clear to those who read these untidy notes of mine.

I would like to speak about everything. But that would not be in accordance with what I wanted—a simple explanation of what seems inexplicable to many persons—and would become an attempt at describing things which cannot really be properly known unless they are seen.

That is why I venture to extend an invitation here to the incredulous to see all that we have done at the *Fundación*, putting into every effort, even the smallest, all the love and all the justice possible.

Of course I only invite those incredulous who are "men of good will"... the incredulous who *wish* to believe... because I know that it is useless to show the others anything; they belong to an ancient breed of mankind, to those who, seeing, do not believe in anything better than mediocrity.

I have no "pearls" to cast before that sort of person...

This part of my notes, written, like all my work, untidily, but with great affection, cannot close without a word of gratitude.

When I think for a moment of all I have to be thankful for, I see clearly that in my work I am... practically nothing.

167

The work was begun because the General inspired me for it and because our *descamisados* demanded it.

Its funds are given me by the people in one way or another.

To erect its buildings, thousands and thousands of laborers work for me, striving as at no other task, and finish their work in extraordinary time, directed by hundreds of technicians who have to be made to rest as though it were an obligation.

Everywhere I find hearts open to collaborate with me, without reserve.

The women who work with me, social service helpers, visitors, nurses, do not know what fatigue and sacrifice mean. Some have already fallen carrying out their duties, as when they went to Ecuador taking help to brethren in that country affected by the earthquake.

The workers of all my country know that the *Fundación* is something belonging to them, and I know that often they send me their generous contributions at a cost which could never be properly rewarded by my work.

I look after these contributions more than my own life . . . and I have promised that the *Fundación* will handle its funds in a crystal casket so that it shall never be soiled with the slightest shadow: that clean money—the only clean money that I know of!—which comes from the workers' honest hands.

For all this I am grateful.

And I even have to thank those who ask for and receive my help, because at times they must possess their souls in patience to come and see me and even to write to me. What I give them is not a favor. What I give them is in payment of an old debt owed them by the country . . . and, this being so, they should not have to ask me for anything! But in practice it always turns out that a larger percentage of those who receive help are those who have asked for it.

I should thank those who are helped because they asked, just as much as those who receive it without asking, for being content with so little. Perón struggles untiringly so that one day nobody on this earth shall have need of social service, which, even carried out as we have wished, with the dignity of justice, is still help . . . And we think that when the world is justicialist, social service too will be a bitter memory!

Every man will have his own.

One day I said this very thing in a speech, and when I had finished speaking, someone near me remarked:

"Perhaps the day when all have their own, and works like yours have disappeared . . . love among men will be a forgotten thing."

I remember answering something more or less like this:

"No. If that day comes sometime . . . I believe that it will never entirely come . . . but if it comes, then the world will be a paradise of love. And if not, see . . . here, in our land, where men are becoming justicialists, see how love triumphs over selfishness. Perón did justice to the workers, and see how the workers give me part of their earnings and of their increases so that I may help the most destitute. I am sure that justice is something like the door of love . . ."

When the world is justicialist, love will reign . . . and so will peace.

Perón taught me this.

It was perhaps his first teaching.

I often wonder why humanity does not also want to learn that marvelous lesson . . . and I feel like going out into the world to preach Perón's justicialism. Anyway, nobody will think I aspire to be an "empress" . . . although many, the mediocre, the average man, the eternally incredulous, would say that I am possessed of a strange form of madness.

But, the "sane" have already accomplished too much in history. And from what one sees, have not given us what we would call a very agreeable world.

Perhaps the turn of the "idealists" has come.

It would be interesting if humanity would give us the opportunity!

46

An Idealist

PERON HIMSELF IS more idealistic—infinitely more idealistic—than am I.

My idealism is only what I have learned from his lessons.

If anything, I was always too practical.

Perón's idealism, on the other hand, is as true as everything about him.

Sometimes I compare him . . . that is to say, I *want* to compare him . . . with someone he resembles.

With Perón, I have read Plutarch's *Parallel Lives of Illustrious Greeks and Romans*.

General Perón likes the life of Alexander.

At first I thought it must be because Alexander was the nearest equivalent to Perón in greatness and in virtue.

That is why I read the life of Alexander with more emotion than any of the other biographies.

Afterward, enthralled by the reading of the great *Lives*, I read many other celebrated biographies.

Perhaps it sounds wrong for me to speak the truth frankly, but I must say what I think, and what I think is easy to say, although everyone may not believe me now . . . at present, although they will believe me afterward, perhaps a long time after we are gone: Perón does not resemble any military genius or politician in history. The military and political geniuses who obtained a little glory, and illuminated a century, won their laurels through the suffering and sacrifice of the people. I do not wish to question their merits in any way, but how many lives did Alexander's glory cost! And how much of the people's blood did Napoleon's glory cost!

And also nobody, absolutely nobody in history, has received so much delirious and fanatical affection as Perón receives . . . and if anyone has received it, none has been able to make better use of it than he for the very happiness of the people.

I think that Perón resembles more another class of geniuses, those who created new philosophies and new religions.

I will not commit the heresy of comparing him with Christ . . . but I am sure that, imitating Christ, Perón feels a profound love for humanity, and that it is this, more than any other thing, which makes him great, magnificently great.

But he is great also because he has known how to put his love into practical form, creating a doctrine so that men should be happy, and carrying it out in our land.

I said that Perón is an idealist, profoundly idealistic. But he is genial, and that is why his idealism is not quixotic, the idealism of a writer or a dreamer.

It is human idealism.

I do not know how he combines all these things.

I see him get an idea sometimes that seems to me to be too far up in the clouds to be carried out. Then I see how this very idea has taken shape . . . and little by little his marvelous hands have turned it into a magnificent reality. He is idealistic and practical at the same time. That is why I firmly believe that he is a genius and that this century will be lighted by him. I see him walking amid a world without faith and without hope, and it seems to me at moments that he is the only thing on earth in which one can still have a little faith and a little hope.

Among those who read this, I know many will smile incredulously. Others will think it propaganda and will turn over the page or close the book. But with some, the thought will remain that perhaps what I say may be the truth.

They will think that, in these moments, so sad and so difficult for mankind, the world appears like an immense battlefield: two small imperialistic minorities, armed as no nations before in history, dispute the right to command an immense humanity which is between two fires, without knowing what to do; it does not want to be communist, it does not want to live in the old ruined capitalistic world.

And no one, except Perón, has anything clear to tell that humanity.

Nobody except Perón shows humanity a new path, giving it new hope. Humanity believes that everything has gone wrong and that there is no remedy for its ills. It even thinks that Christianity itself has failed . . . and Perón tells it frankly:

"No. What has failed is not Christianity. It is man who has failed by applying it wrongly. Christianity has never yet been properly tried by man, because the world has never been just. Christianity will come true when love reigns among men and among the peoples; but love can only come when men and the peoples are justicialists."

Yes. Perhaps it is too idealistic.

But . . . the world needs hope. And hope is always this: a remote idea . . . which God mysteriously converts into reality!

PART THREE
Women and My Mission

47

Women and My Mission

MY WORK IN the woman's movement began and grew, just like my work of social service and my trade-union activities, little by little, and more by force of circumstances than through any decision of mine.

This may not be what many imagine to be the case, but it is the truth.

It would be more romantic or more poetic or more literary, and more like fiction, if I said, for example, that all I do now I had felt intuitively . . . as a vocation or a special decree of fate.

But such is not the case.

All I brought by way of preparation to the scene of these struggles were those same *feelings* which had made me think of the problem of the rich and the poor.

But nothing more.

I never imagined it would fall to my lot someday to lead a woman's movement in my country, and still less a political movement.

Circumstances showed the way.

Ah! But I did not remain in my comfortable position of Eva Perón. The path which opened up before my eyes was the path I took if by it I could help Perón's cause a little—the cause of the people.

177

I imagine many other women have seen the paths I pursue long before I did.

The only difference between them and me is that they stayed behind and I started. Actually, I should confess that if I girded myself for a struggle it was not for myself but for him . . . for Perón!

He encouraged me to rise.

He took me out of "the flock of sparrows."

He taught me my first steps in all my undertakings.

Afterward I never lacked the powerful and extraordinary stimulus of his love.

I realize, above all, that I began my work in a woman's movement because Perón's cause demanded it.

It all began little by little.

Before I realized it I was already heading a woman's political movement . . . and, with it, had to accept the spiritual leadership of the women of my country.

This caused me to meditate on woman's problems. And, more than that, to feel them, and to feel them in the light of the doctrine with which Perón was beginning to build a New Argentina.

I remember with what extraordinary fondness, as friend and master, General Perón explained to me innumerable women's problems in my country and in the world.

In these conversations I again became aware of the kindliness of his nature.

Millions of men have faced, as he has faced, the ever more acute problem of woman's role in humanity in this afflicted century; but I think very few of them have stopped, like Perón, to penetrate it to its depths.

In this, as in everything, he showed me the way.

The world's feminists will say that to start a woman's movement in this way is hardly feministic . . . to start by recognizing to a certain extent the superiority of a man!

However, I am not interested in criticisms.

Also, recognizing Perón's superiority is a different matter.

Besides . . . it is my intention to write the truth.

48

From the Sublime to
The Ridiculous

I CONFESS I was a little afraid the day I found myself facing the possibility of starting on the "feminist" path.

What could I, a humble woman of the people, do where other women, more prepared than I, had categorically failed?

Be ridiculous? Join the nucleus of women with a grudge against woman and against man, as has happened to innumerable feminist leaders?

I was not an old maid, nor even ugly enough for such a post . . . which, from the time of the English suffragettes down to today, generally belongs, almost exclusively, to women of this type . . . women whose first impulse undoubtedly had been to be like men.

And that is how they guided the movements they led!

They seemed to be dominated by indignation at not having been born men, more than by the pride of being women.

They thought, too, that it was a misfortune to be a woman. They were resentful of women who did not want to stop being women. They were resentful of men because they would not let them be like them; the "feminists," the immense majority of feminists in the world, as far as I could see, continued to be a strange species of woman . . . which never seemed to me to be entirely womanly!

And I did not feel very much inclined to be like them.

One day the General gave me the explanation I needed.

"Don't you see that they have missed the way? They want to be men. It is as though to save the workers I had tried to make oligarchs of them. I would have remained without workers. And I do not think I should have managed to improve the oligarchy at all. Don't you see that this class of 'feminists' detests womanhood? Some of them do not even use makeup . . . because that, according to them, is womanly. Don't you see they want to be men? And if what the world requires is a woman's political and social movement . . . how little will the world gain if the women want to save it by imitating men! We have done too many strange things and made such a mess of everything that I do not know if the world can be arranged anew. Perhaps woman can save us, on condition that she does not imitate us."

I well remember that lesson of the General's.

His ideas never seemed to me so clear and bright.

That is how I felt.

I felt that the woman's movement in my country and all over the world had to fulfill a sublime mission . . . and everything I knew about feminism seemed to me ridiculous. For, not led by women but by those who aspired to be men, it ceased to be womanly and was nothing! Feminism had taken the step from the sublime to the ridiculous.

And that is the step I always try to avoid taking!

49

I Would Like to Show
Them a Way

THE FIRST THING I had to do in my country's woman's movement was to solve the old problem of woman's political rights.

For a century—the dark and painful century of selfish oligarchy and those who sold their country—politicians of every party had often promised woman the vote. Promises which were never made good, like all those they made to the people.

Perhaps that was lucky.

If women had begun to vote in the days of the oligarchy, the disillusion would have been too great . . . as great as the deceit of those elections in which all misconduct, all fraud and all lies were normal!

It was better for us to have no rights then. Now we have an advantage over men. We have not been mocked! We have not joined any strange political confabulation! The struggle for ambition has not touched us. And, above all, we are born to civic life under Perón's banner, whose elections are a model of integrity and honesty, as is admitted by even his most venomous adversaries, who surrender to the truth only when it is impossible to invent one more lie.

Today the Argentine woman may vote. I am not going to

repeat the expression used by a politician who, on offering his fellow citizens an electoral law, stated too solemnly:

"Let the people know how to vote!"

No. I think the people always knew *how* to vote. The trouble is that it was not always possible for them to vote. The same thing happens with woman.

And she will know how to vote. Although it is not fundamental in the feminist movement, the vote is its most powerful instrument, and with it we women of all the world have to win all our rights . . . or, rather, the great right of being simply *women*, and thus being able to fulfill, totally and absolutely, the mission that, as women, we have to perform for humanity.

What I think we cannot ever forget is a thing Perón always repeats to the men: that the vote, that is to say, "politics," is not an end but a means.

I think that men, in their great majority, above all in the old political parties, never understood this properly. That is why they always failed. Our destiny as women depends on our not falling into the same error.

But I do not want to linger longer on this matter of woman's political rights.

I am more interested at present in woman herself.

I would like to show her a way.

50

Home or the Factory?

EVERY DAY THOUSANDS of women forsake the feminine camp and begin to live like men.

They work like them. They prefer, like them, the street to the home. They are not resigned to being either mothers or wives.

They substitute for men everywhere.

Is this "feminism"? I think, rather, that it must be the "masculinization" of our sex.

And I wonder if all this change has solved our problem.

But no. All the old ills continue rampant, and new ones, too, appear. The number of young women who look down upon the occupation of homemaking increases every day.

And yet that is what we were born for.

We feel that we are born for the home, and the home is too great a burden for our shoulders.

Then we give up the home . . . go out to find a solution . . . feel that the answer lies in obtaining economic independence and working somewhere. But that work makes us equal to men and—no! We are not like them! They can live alone; we cannot. We feel the need of company, of complete company. We feel the need of giving more than receiving. Can't we work for anything else than earning wages like men?

And, on the other hand, if we give up the work which makes

us independent so as to form a home . . . we burn our boats once and for all.

No profession in the world has less chance of a comeback than our profession as women.

Even if we are chosen by a good man, our home will not always be what we dreamed of when we were single.

The entire nation ends at the door of our home, and other laws and other rights begin . . . the law and the rights of man— who very often is only a master, and also, at times, a dictator.

And nobody can interfere there.

The mother of a family is left out of all security measures. She is the only worker in the world without a salary, or a guarantee, or limited working hours, or free Sundays, or holidays, or any rest, or indemnity for dismissal, or strikes of any kind. All that, we learned as girls, belongs to the sphere of love . . . but the trouble is that after marriage, love often flies out of the window, and then everything becomes "forced labor" . . . obligations without any rights! Free service in exchange for pain and sacrifice!

I do not say it is always like this. I should have no right to say anything, since *my* home is happy . . . if I did not see the suffering every day of so many women who live like that . . . with no outlook, with no rights, with no hope.

That is why every day there are fewer women to make homes.

Real homes, united and happy! And the world really needs more homes every day, and for them more women willing properly to fulfill their destiny and their mission. That is why the first objective of a feminine movement which wishes to improve things for women—which does not aim at changing them into men—should be the home.

We were born to make homes. Not for the street. Common sense shows us the answer. We must have in the home that which we go out to seek: our small economic independence—which would save us from becoming women with no outlook, with no rights and with no hope!

51
An Idea

FOR IN REALITY the same thing must happen with women as with men, families and nations: as long as they are not economically independent, no one concedes them any rights.

I imagine many persons will see too material an outlook in this very personal opinion, very much my own.

And this is not so. I believe in spiritual values. Also, this is what Perón's justicialist doctrine teaches us. That is just why—because I believe in the spirit—I consider it urgent to reconcile in woman her need to be a wife and mother with the other needs which as a worthy human being she also carries in her innermost heart.

And the first thing in solving the problem, I think, would be the small economic independence of which I have spoken.

If we do not find an answer to our dilemma, an inconceivable thing will soon happen in the world. Only the less capable women will be willing to form a real home (not half a home, or half a marriage) . . . those who cannot find any other "economic" way to sustain their minimum rights except by marriage and the home.

The status of mother of a family will come down to a ridiculous level. It will be said—and it is already being said—that only fools burn their boats by getting married, building a home, burdening themselves with children.

And can that not happen in the world?

It is the moral values which have been shattered by this disastrous state of affairs; and it will not be the men who will restore them to their old prestige, nor will it be the masculine women either. No. Will it, perhaps, be the mothers?

I do not know how to prove this, but I feel it is the absolute truth.

But how can one reconcile all these things?

To me it seems very simple, and I do not know if it is not too simple and, perhaps, impracticable; although I have often noticed how things we consider too simple are often the key to success, the secret of victory.

I think one should commence by fixing a small monthly allowance for every woman who gets married, from the day of her marriage.

A salary paid to the mothers by all the nation and which comes out of all the earnings of all the workers in the country, including the women.

Nobody will say that it is not just for us to pay for the work which, even if it is not seen, demands the efforts of millions and millions of women whose time, whose lives, are spent on this monotonous but heavy task of cleaning the house, looking after clothes, laying the table, bringing up children, etc.

That allowance could be, for a start, half the average national salary, and thus the woman, housekeeper, mistress of the home, would have an income of her own apart from what the man wishes to give her.

Later increases for each child could be added to this basic salary, an increase in case of widowhood, lost if she joins the ranks of the workers—in a word, in all the ways likely to be of most help so that the original purpose shall not be lost sight of.

I only suggest the idea. If it is suitable, it would have to be given shape and converted into actual fact.

I know that for us, the women of my country, the problem is not serious or urgent.

That is why I do not yet wish to carry this idea into the field of action. It would be better for everyone to think it over. When the time comes, the idea should be ripe.

I offer this solution so that the woman who starts a home shall not feel herself below the woman who earns her living in a factory or in an office.

But it does not solve entirely the old problem. A better use of progress and of the technique of running a home must be added.

And to attain this, it is necessary to raise woman's general level of culture. Economic independence and technical progress should be used in behalf of her rights and of her freedom, without losing sight of her marvelous status as a woman: the one thing which cannot and should not be lost sight of unless one does not want to lose everything.

All this reminds me a little of Perón's basic program in his struggle for the freedom of the workers.

He used to say it was necessary to raise the level of social culture, dignify work and humanize capital.

I, imitating him always, suggest that to save woman, and at the same time the home, it is necessary also to raise the level of woman's culture, dignify her work and humanize her economy by giving her a certain minimum material independence.

Only thus can woman prepare herslf to be a wife and mother, just as she prepares herself to be a shorthand-typist.

In this way many women would be saved from the delinquency and prostitution which are the fruits of their economic slavery.

In this way the prestige of the home would be saved and kept really sacred as the foundation stone of humanity.

I know my solution is more a remedy than a solution. I know it is only a beginning, a gesture. I think a great deal more will still have to be done.

Because it is not a matter of trying to return to the home a prestige it is losing, but of giving it an entirely new one.

I have had to create many institutions where children were to be looked after, trying to substitute something for which there is no substitute: a mother and a home. But I dream of the day when institutions will no longer be necessary, when woman will be what she ought to be—queen and mistress of a worthy family, free from the pressures of economic needs.

To bring about that day, and that justicialism in all its aspects may be a reality everywhere, the woman's movement of every country and of the whole world must unite. A woman's movement organized in a world without social justice would be of no value to us.

It would be like a great workers' movement in a world without work. It would be no good whatever!

52

The Great Absence

I THINK THE feminist movement organized as a vital force in each country and in all the world should and would do great good to all humanity.

I do not know where I once read that in this world of ours the great need is for love.

I would modify this a bit and say that rather does the world today suffer from a great absence: that of woman.

Everything, absolutely everything in this contemporary world, has been made according to man's measure.

We are absent from governments.

We are absent from parliaments.

From international organizations.

We are in neither the Vatican nor the Kremlin.

Nor in the high commands of the imperialists.

Nor in the commissions of atomic energy.

Nor in the great business combines.

Nor in Freemasonry, nor in other secret societies.

We are absent from all the great centers constituting a power in the world.

And yet we have always been present in the time of suffering, and in all humanity's bitter hours.

It would seem as though our calling were not substantially

that of creating, but rather that of sacrifice.

Our symbol should be of the Mother of Christ at the foot of the Cross.

And yet our highest mission is nothing but to create.

I cannot understand, then, why we are not in those places where an attempt is being made to create man's happiness.

Haven't we, by any chance, a common destiny with man? Shouldn't we perhaps share in creating the happiness of the family?

Perhaps man has failed in his attempts thus far to make mankind happy, precisely *because* he has not invited us to join his great social organizations.

To solve the serious problems of the world, man has created an almost unlimited series of doctrines.

He has created a doctrine for each century.

And after this has been tried and has failed, he has tried another, and so on.

He has been inspired by each doctrine as though it were a definite solution. The doctrine has been more important to him than man or humanity.

And the reason is this: man has no *personal* stake in humanity, as women have.

To man humanity is a social, economic and political problem.

To us humanity is a problem of creation . . . just as every woman and every man represents our suffering and our sacrifice.

Man accepts too easily the destruction of another man or of a woman, of an aged person or a child.

He does not know what it costs to create them!

We do!

That is why we, the women of all the earth, have, in addition to our creative calling, another and allied calling, that of instinctive preservation; in other words, the sublime calling of peace.

By this I do not mean to say that we should prefer "peace at any price."

No. We know there are more important motives than peace, but they are less important to us than they are to man.

We do not understand waging war for imperialism, and still less for economic superiority; we do not understand war as a means of conquest.

Although we do know that there are wars of justice, we think that, up to the present, men have fought very little for that justice.

When man gives us a place in his supreme decisions, the hour will have come to assert our opinion, less from the head perhaps than from the heart.

But is it not our hearts that have to suffer the consequences of the errors of the "brains" of men?

I do not despise man or his intelligence, but if in many parts of the world we have created happy homes together, why cannot we create a happy humanity together?

That ought to be our objective.

Nothing more than to win the right to create—together with man—something better than we now have.

53

The Peronista Feminist Party

THE WOMAN'S PARTY led by me in my country is linked logically to the Peronista movement, but is independent, as a party, from that formed by men.

I have arranged this on purpose, so that the women may not become masculine in their political eagerness.

Just as the workers could save themselves only by their own efforts, and, as I have always said, repeating Perón, that "only the humble will save the humble," I also think that only women can be the salvation of women.

In that lies the cause of my decision to organize the feminist party apart from the Peronista men's political organization.

We are completely united by the one and undisputed Leader of all.

We are united by the great objectives of the Peronista doctrine and movement.

And there is only one thing to separate us: we have an objective of our own, and that is to redeem woman.

This objective is contained in Perón's justicialist doctrine, but it is up to us women to attain it.

For this we also ought to win beforehand the effective collaboration of the men.

I am optimistic about it. The men of Peronism who gave us

193

the right to vote are not likely to remain behind now . . .

I found the organizing of the woman's party one of the most difficult undertakings that has fallen to my lot.

With no precedent in the country—I think this has been my good luck—and with no resources except the spirit put to the service of a great cause, one day I called together a small group of women.

There were hardly thirty of them.

All were very young. I had known them as my indefatigable collaborators in social welfare, as fervent Peronistas on all occasions, as fanatics in the cause of Perón.

I had to demand great sacrifices of them: to leave their homes, their work, practically to leave one entire life so as to begin a different one, hard and intense.

For that I needed women like this, indefatigable, fervent, fanatical.

It was indispensable above all to take a census of all the women throughout the length and breadth of the country who felt our Peronista faith.

That undertaking required intrepid women willing to work day and night.

Out of those thirty women with no other ambition than that of serving the justicialist cause, only a very few failed me.

Therefore I say that by choosing them for their love of the cause more than for other reasons, I chose well.

We are still working as on the first day.

It delights me to follow the progress of the movement from near at hand. What is important is to preserve intact the stamp of femininity which I wished to instill in them.

This occasioned some difficulties at the start.

In isolated zones of the country there were a few political "bosses"—happily very few remain now in the Peronista movement; the majority are in the old opposition parties—who believed in making the feminist movement a thing of their own which should come under their management and suggestions.

My "girls" behaved magnificently, preserving their independence of opinion and action.

This made me realize that my lengthy instructions to that first initial group had been well learned.

And that in its political activities the feminist movement had started well and was beginning to progress by itself.

Today, all over the country, thousands and thousands of women work actively for the organization.

With the full powers extended to me by the First National Assembly, I was able to direct all the work of the organization freely.

This means many hours of patient work for me in meetings, personal conversations with censor delegates, a few disappointments, many difficulties, but . . . all is compensated by the joy I feel when on our special days I can go to the Leader with my women and report to him on our progress and triumphs.

The political centers of the feminist party are called "basic units."

In this we have wished to imitate the men.

But I am much afraid that our basic units are nearer to Perón's original concept, when he first advised having them as fundamental elements of the men's political organization.

The General did not wish the men of his political party to set up the old, despised "committees" which in the oligarchic political organizations so long endured by the country were dens of vice opened for each election in all districts and towns.

Perón wanted ours—the Peronista political centers—to be centers of culture and useful activities for the Argentines.

My centers, my basic units, fulfill that wish of Perón's.

Libraries are organized in the units, cultural lectures are given, and, although I did not establish it expressly, they were early converted into centers of help and of social welfare.

The *descamisados* still do not distinguish between the political organization of which I am the head, and the work of my *Fundación*.

The basic units to them are something of "Evita's." And they go there looking for what they expect "Evita" may give them.

They themselves, my *descamisados*, are those who have created a new function in my basic units: that of informing the *Fundación* concerning the needs of all the humble of the country. The *Fundación* attends to these requests by sending them its help directly.

I have been severely criticized for this. My unrelenting critics consider that in this way I use my *Fundación* for political ends.

And . . . perhaps they are right! What appears to be the final consequence of my work is its political repercussion. People see in my work the hand of Perón extending to the farthest corner of my country . . . and that cannot be pleasing to his enemies.

But . . . can I turn a deaf ear to the clamor of the humble, whatever the means by which it reaches me?

If at any time the parties opposed to Perón sent me a request from some *descamisado*, the *Fundación* would also give its succor where it was required.

Has the *Fundación* by any chance ever asked the name, race, religion or party of anyone it helps?

But I am sure no oligarch would ever make me such a request.

They were not born to ask.

And still less to ask on behalf of the misery of the humble . . .!

To them that savors of melodrama . . . the melodrama of the rabble which they despised from their balconies with the insult which is our glory: *Descamisados*!

54

Let Them Bark!

LET THEM BARK!

Every time they bark, we win.

What would be harmful would be for them to applaud! In this connection, very often it is evident that some of our own workers preserve their old prejudices.

They are apt to say, for example:

"Even the opposition approved!"

They do not realize that here, in our country, to say "opposition" still means the same as saying "oligarchy." . . . And that is equivalent to our saying "enemies of the people."

If they agree with us, look out! The people are not likely to be in agreement.

I would like each Peronista to carve this thought on his innermost heart, because it is fundamental for the movement.

Nothing belonging to the oligarchy can be good!

I do not say that some oligarch or other may not do something good. It is unlikely, but if it happened I think it would be by mistake. It would be as well to warn him that he is turning Peronista!

And mark, when I speak of the oligarchy I refer to all those who in 1946 opposed Perón—conservatives, radicals, socialists and communists. All voted for the Argentina of the old oligarchic surrendering and country-selling regime.

They will never be able to redeem that sin.

Many persons abroad do not understand sometimes that Perón is unconditional in his irrevocable decision to work with his own party, and that he always attacks his opponents, sometimes even harshly.

Accustomed to the policy of collaboration which in other countries is almost a habit, our vigorous and definite division is not understood.

Many persons ignore the numerous times Perón invited his enemies to collaborate honestly.

I know that he appealed to them sincerely.

But I also know that he appealed to them without any hope.

He knew them before I did, and even better than I do.

They are incapable of generosity. They do not think of anything but themselves.

The nation, to them, was always a name, the name of a commodity to be sold to the highest bidder!

That is why the General governs as if they did not exist. If he remembers them and attacks them, it is only so that the people may not forget that they are still the same who, in 1946, surrendered themselves to a foreign ambassador.

Luckily for the Argentines, they belong to a breed of men which will come to an end in this century . . . with the generation to which they belong.

Not even their children will want to remember them!

55
Women and Action

I FIRMLY BELIEVE that woman—contrary to the common opinion held by men—lives better in action than in inactivity.

I see them every day in my work of political service and social welfare.

The reason is very simple. Man can live exclusively for himself. Woman cannot.

If a woman lives for herself, I think she is not a woman, or else she cannot be said to live. That is why I am afraid of the "masculinization" of women.

When that occurs, women become even more egoistic than men, because we women carry things to greater extremes than men.

A man of action is one who triumphs over all the rest. A woman of action is one who triumphs *for* the rest. Isn't this a great difference?

Woman's happiness is not her own happiness, but that of others.

That is why, when I thought of my feminist movement, I did not want to take woman out of what is so much her own sphere. In politics men seek their own triumph.

Women, if they did that, would cease to be women.

I have not wanted women to look to themselves in the

woman's party . . . but rather that right there they should serve others in some fraternal and generous form.

Woman's problem everywhere is always the deep and fundamental problem of the home.

It is her great destiny—her irremediable destiny.

She needs to have a home; when she cannot make one with her own flesh, she does so with her soul, or she is not a woman!

Well, for this very reason I have wanted my party to be a home . . . that each basic unit should be something like a family . . . with its great loves and its small disagreements, with its sublime fruitfulness and its interminable laboriousness.

I know that in many places I have already attained this.

Above all, where the women I have appointed are most womanly!

More than political action, the feminist movement has to develop social service. Precisely because social service is something that we women have in the blood!

Our destiny and our vocation is to serve others, and that is social service.

Not that other "social life" . . . which is contrary to *all* service . . .!

56
Social Life

MAY I SAY a few words about "social life"?

I have said worse things in my life!

I believe that "social life," like the aristocratic and bourgeois society that lives it, are two things that are coming to an end. This century will finish them both!

I never understood women of that class of empty and easy living, nor do I think they ever understand any other kind of life.

They belong to another breed of women. To say they are like men would be an insult which men do not deserve.

Real man, and real woman, though different, each lives for something. Each has an object in life, and each performs it as best he or she can.

The "society woman" is not like that, because social life has no object. It is full of appearances, of trivialities, of mediocrities and of lies. Everything consists of acting well a silly and ridiculous part.

In the theater, at least, something that once existed or which may exist is represented. In the theater, the actor knows he is someone. In social life, women are actresses representing— what? Nothing, absolutely nothing! I never envied or liked that kind of actor.

But I understand them. It is very easy to understand what

201

happens. It is very difficult to fill up a life when one has no object. Then one has to fill up the days and nights with that collection of minor and unimportant things that make up "social life."

And once they are accustomed to that, everything else seems to them ridiculous and extravagant.

To the sparrows, the flight of the condors must seem like that!

One cannot speak to that class of women of anything great and different. The home, to them, is secondary; to put it first would mean the sacrifice of all that composes "social life"—its parties, its gatherings, bridge, the races, etc. It is as though they had been born for all these things, and not to serve as a bridge for humanity. They do not know that humanity passes from one generation to another through our bodies and our souls, and that for this reason it is necessary for each one of us to make a home.

Neither do they understand the suffering of the humble. When some news of that great human suffering reaches them, they may cry a little . . . but the tears end in a charity entertainment. This kind of woman knows, however, in her innermost heart, that the life she lives is not real.

It is said that through its social life one may come to know the culture of a people. I protest indignantly against such a stupid statement.

Yes, I know that it is very much "the thing" to call oneself cultured . . . and it is very "good class" to receive in one's midst intellectuals, thinkers, poets, artists, etc.

This is a hospitable, patronizing and attractive function, and it is very understandable that intellectuals feel attracted and flattered by the attentions and the material luxury of "good society."

They do not realize that generally they play a silly and ridiculous role in it. They are the *compères* of a theatrical piece which in itself has no means of entertaining anyone.

And in that consists the culture of "social life."

57

The Woman Who Was
Not Praised

THAT IS WHY, perhaps, writers and poets have said so much about beautiful and elegant women . . . and have sung woman's praises, seeing only that class of woman whose femininity is unquestioned.

That is why writers and poets have not expressed the real truth about woman.

Woman is not like that. She is not empty, light, superficial and vain. She is not, as they have written, selfish, fatal and romantic.

No. She is not, as they have painted her, gossiping and envious.

They saw her thus because they were not able to see the genuine woman who, precisely because she is genuine, takes silent refuge in the homes of the people where humanity is eternal.

That woman has not been acclaimed by the intellectuals.

She has no history. She gives no receptions. She does not play bridge.

She does not smoke. She does not go to the races.

She is the unknown heroine. Unknown even to her husband!

Even to her children.

Of her nothing elegant, nothing clever, will ever be written.

At the most, after her death, her children will say:

"Now we realize all she meant to us."

And that tardy lament will be her only praise.

That is why I have wanted to say all these things. This is my way of paying my tribute, the highest tribute of my heart, to the genuine woman who lives among the people and who creates every day a little of the people.

It is she who constitutes the great object of my solicitude.

I know that she, only she, holds the future of the people in her hands. The new humanity required by Perón's justicialism will be formed not so much in the schools as in the home.

That is why I am anxious that the genuine woman of the people shall make herself capable in every sense . . . because school is like one of those workshops where pictures are painted in a series . . . but the home is an artist's workshop in which each picture is a little of its soul and of its life.

It is there that exceptional men and women are fashioned.

The new justicialist age which we are starting needs many such men and women.

And in spite of every effort, we cannot offer them to humanity if they are not bred for us by women of the genuine people, enamored of Perón's cause, zealously instructed and capable.

That is just why I think it better to instruct, prepare and educate a woman than a man. The moment has come to give greater importance to the miracle by which every day we women, in a certain sense, create the destiny of the world!

And with all the more reason now, when men have lost faith. . . . We never lose faith. And we know well that, when everything is lost, all can be saved if something is kept, even if it be a little faith.

58

Like Any Other Woman

ALL I WANTED to say is now said.

I am nothing more than a humble woman of a great people . . . like all the peoples of the earth!

A woman like whom there are thousands and thousands in the world. God chose me from among so many and put me in this position close to the Leader of a new world: Perón.

Why was I chosen and not another?

I do not know.

But what I did and what I do is what any woman would do, out of the immense number of women of this people of ours, or of any people in the world, who know how to fulfill their destiny as women, silently, in the fruitful solitude of the home.

I feel nothing more than the humble representative of all the women of the people.

I feel, like them, that I am the head of a home, much larger, it is true, than those they have made, but in the final count a home: the prosperous home of this country of mine which Perón is leading toward its very highest destinies.

Thanks to him, the "home," which at first was poor and dismantled, is now just, free and sovereign!

He did it all!

His wonderful hands converted each hope of our people into

205

thousands of realities.

Now we live happily, with that happiness of a home, sprinkled with work and even a little bitterness . . . which form a little part of the fabric of happiness.

In this great home of the nation I am like a woman of any of the countless homes of my people.

Like her I am, after all, a woman.

I like the same things that she does: jewels and furs, dresses and shoes . . . but, like her, I prefer everyone in the home to be better off than I am. Like her, like all of her prototypes, I would like to be free to go out and enjoy myself . . . but I am tied, like her, to the duties of the home which no one else is obliged to do in my place.

Like all of them, I get up early thinking of my husband and of my children . . . and thinking of them I go about all day and a good deal of the night. . . . When I go to bed, tired, my dreams are lost in wonderful schemes, and I try to fall asleep before the spell is broken.

Like all of them, I awake startled by the slightest noise, because, like all of them, I am also frightened . . .

Like them I always like to appear smiling and attractive to my husband and my children, always serene and strong so as to inspire them with faith and hope . . . and, like them, I am also at times overcome by difficulties, and like them, I shut myself up and cry and cry!

Like all of them I prefer my smallest and weakest children . . . and love those who have least best. . . .

Like all women of all the homes of my people, my joyful days are those when all the children, happy and affectionate, are gathered round the head of the house.

Like them, I know that the children of this great house which is the nation need me and my husband . . . and I try to see that they are not disappointed.

I like, as they do, preparing agreeable surprises and enjoying the surprise of my husband and my children afterward.

Like them, I hide my disappointments and troubles, and often appear bright and happy to my family, while hiding the grief which makes my heart bleed with a smile and with my words.

I hear, as they do, as do all the mothers in all the homes of my people, the advice of visitors and of friends: "But why do you take things so seriously?" "Don't worry so much!" "Enjoy yourself a bit more! Why do you want more than all the pretty things you have in your wardrobe?"

The thing is that, like them, I like looking nice more among my own than before strangers . . . and that is why I wear my best finery when I attend to the *descamisados*.

Very often I think, as they do, of going on holidays, of traveling, of knowing the world . . . but I am prevented by the thought: "If I go, who will do my work?" And I stay!

For I really feel myself the mother of my people!

And I honestly think that I am.

Do I not suffer with it? Do I not rejoice in its joys? Do not its sorrows hurt me? Do I not feel my blood rise when they are insulted or criticized?

My loves are their loves.

That is why I love Perón now in a different way from before: before I loved him for himself . . . now I also love him because my people love him!

For all these reasons, because I feel myself one of so many women of the people building up the happiness of their homes, and because I have reached that happiness, I desire it for all and every one of these women of my people.

I want them to be as happy in their homes as I am in this great home which is my country.

When destiny once more chooses a woman for this highest national home, I want any woman of my people to be able to fill, better than I do, this mission that I perform as best I can.

Until the last day of my life I want to fulfill the great task of opening new horizons and paths for my *descamisados*, for my workers, for my women.

I know that, like any woman of the people, I am stronger than I appear to be, and my health is better than the doctors think.

Like her, like all of them, I am ready to go on struggling so that there will always be happiness in my great home.

I do not aspire to any honor that is not that happiness!

That is my vocation and my destiny.

That is my mission.

Like any woman of my people, I want to perform it well and to the end.

Perhaps someday when I am gone for good, someone will say of me what so many children of the people are wont to say when their mothers have gone, also for good:

Only now do we realize that she loved us so much!

59

I Am Not Sorry

I THINK I have already written too much.

I only wanted to explain myself, and I think that perhaps I have only half done so.

But it would be useless to go on writing. Those who have not understood me up to this, who have not *heard* me, would not hear me even if I continued these jottings for another thousand pages.

I see here now at my side really piles of paper exhausted with my large handwriting . . . and I think the moment has come to finish.

I read the first pages . . . and go revising all I have written.

I know that I should not have said many things . . . If at any time they are read through historical curiosity, they will not do me much good: people will say, for example, that I was too cruel to Perón's enemies.

But . . . I have not written this for history.

All has been done for this extraordinary and wonderful present time in which my lot has fallen: for my people and for all the souls in the world who feel, from near or far, that a new day for humanity is about to dawn: the day of justicialism.

I have only wanted to announce it in my good or poor language . . . in the same words that I announce it every day to the men and women of my own people.

I am not sorry for a word that I have written. They would first have to be wiped out of the soul of my people, which has heard them from me so often and because of that offered me its unparalleled affection.

An affection worth more than my life!

Appendix I

Juan Peron's was a career that seesawed between the zenith of power and oblivion. And on each occasion the guiding hand of Eva, first as his mistress, then as his wife, finally as the insistent wraith of *Evita*, lifted him out of the abyss.

She organized the workers' revolt that secured his freedom in 1945 and swept him to the Presidency a year later. Her mesmeric oratory gave the General a second term in office; her memory brought the aged dictator out of exile after eighteen years and, ironically, allowed his new wife to become the first woman President in history.

MONDAY AUGUST 6 1945

CRITICS OF COL. PERON IN ARGENTINA

SERVICE LEADERS' REQUEST

FROM OUR OWN CORRESPONDENT
BUENOS AIRES, Aug. 5

The resignation of Colonel Peron, the Argentine Vice-President, War Minister, and Secretary of Labour and Welfare, was implicitly demanded in a six-point document recently submitted by 11 admirals and 30 generals to President Farrell and published to-day.

The document stated that the signatories did not claim to support or veto Presidential candidates, but considered that political propaganda should not be carried on by holders of public office. Any office holder intending to become a Presidential candidate or whom circumstances suggested as a candidate should resign from the Government.

It is officially stated that General Farrell verbally invited military and naval leaders to express their views patriotically and frankly on the Argentine political situation, especially in connexion with the elections which General Farrell recently promised.

ARGENTINE PRESIDENT'S PROMOTION

FROM OUR OWN CORRESPONDENT
BUENOS AIRES, Aug. 9

President Farrell, who is leaving Buenos Aires to-morrow on an official visit to Paraguay, to return the visit which the Paraguayan President, General Morinigo, made to Argentina in 1943, to-day delegated the Presidential powers during his absence to the Vice-President, Colonel Peron. The first deed of Colonel Peron as acting President of Argentina was to issue a decree promoting President Farrell from Brigadier-General to the rank of divisional general, which caused some surprise, although President Farrell is due for promotion.

MORE RIOTING IN BUENOS AIRES

TWO PERSONS KILLED

FROM OUR OWN CORRESPONDENT
BUENOS AIRES, Aug. 16

Rioting again occurred in the centr streets of Buenos Aires last night, and tw more persons were killed and mar injured.

Groups hostile to the Government, large composed of students and Communists, chee ing for democracy, clashed with rival grou shouting for the acting President, Colon Peron. Colonel Peron's men were reinforc by many soldiers in uniform and wearing sid arms.

An unsuccessful attempt was made wi bottles of petrol to set fire to the premis of the *Critica*, a democratic and popular afte noon newspaper, after the building had be stoned. About 1,000 Government supporte including soldiers, are reported to have e changed shots with the occupants of building, and it was here that the two deat and most of the casualties occurred. La the police surrounded the *Critica* buildi alleging that the first shots came from inside.

A procession of Colonel Peron's supporte headed by soldiers with drawn bayone marched through the Calle Florida, the ch shopping street, and further clashes occurr many windows being broken. Later Gove ment House was stoned by democrats. Duri most of the rioting no police were visible.

The nationalist organization, Alianza Lib tadora Nacionalista, announced that their su porters had not taken part in the demonst tions or counter-demonstrations because th were entirely out of sympathy with both sid

FRIDAY AUGUST 17 194

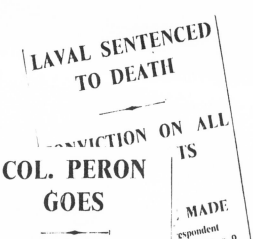

LAVAL SENTENCED TO DEATH

◀▬ONVICTION ON ALL ▬▬TS

▬▬ MADE

espondent

COL. PERON GOES

SUDDEN LOSS OF OFFICE

MOVE BY ARGENTINE MILITARY

From Our Own Correspondent

BUENOS AIRES, Oct. 9

Colonel Juan Peron, the Argentine ice-President, War Minister, Secretary Labour and Welfare, and president of e post-war council, who has been the untry's strong man since the military volution of June 4, 1943, to-day resigned l his posts in the Government. The nouncement was made to the Press by e Minister of the Interior, Dr. Quijano, ter a day of wildest rumours. Dr. uijano added that the Government had -day resolved to call elections for next pril, and that at his request the decree nvoking them would be signed on ctober 12, the anniversary of the discovery of America.

Colonel Peron's sudden fall from power as caused when officers at the military se at the Campo de Mayo turned against m and all his appeals to General luardo Avalos, commanding the garrin, proved to be in vain. Rioting began the streets of Buenos Aires as soon as e news of the resignation became known, any citizens displaying the utmost joy.

The resignation does not necessarily indicate or even suggest that Colonel Peron intends to withdraw from public life. On the contrary, out of office he could prepare his candidature, if not more freely, at least with more justification. It is recalled that the Army and Navy leaders, when President Farrell consulted them, implicitly asked for Colonel Peron's resignation. Colonel Peron undoubtedly has Presidential ambitions, and in a recent speech he admitted he was ambitious, but ambitious to secure social and economic benefits for the Argentine working and peasant classes. On that occasion he surprised many people by referring to the Argentine nation as " my people "—like a king or an emperor. Many Argentines disapproved of this, saying to each other: " We aren't anybody's people."

RELATIONS WITH U.S.

It is expected that Colonel Peron's resignation will ease the crisis in the relations between Argentina and the United States, the extreme gravity of which is fully realized in Argentina in spite of the muzzling effect of the state of siege. It was felt that if something did not happen soon to improve the situation blood would inevitably flow. How much support Colonel Peron enjoys among the workers nobody knows, because there has never been any test, though Colonel Peron once boasted that 4,000,000 Argentine workers were ready to die for him. It is known that the Argentines of property loathe him.

The crisis in Argentine affairs, which has been developing for a long time, was brought to a head by an open clash between the Executive and the Legislature when the Government arrested a Judge and the Supreme Court declared the Government's decision illegal.

BUENOS AIRES, Oct. 9.— Earlier to-day General Avalos was reported to have sent Colonel Peron an ultimatum giving him until 6 o'clock to-night to resign. In the afternoon troops began to march on Buenos Aires, and the Ministry of War was taken over by General Avalos's men.—*Reuter.*

HE TIMES WEDNESDAY OCTOBER 10 1945

FULL POWER FOR PERON

PRESIDENT'S OFFER

BUENOS AIRES IN TUMULT

From Our Own Correspondent
BUENOS AIRES, Oct. 17

Many thousands of workers are reported to be marching to Government House from all parts of Buenos Aires in support of Colonel Peron, the ex-Vice President. One column is said to be over half a mile long, while another comprises 10,000 persons.

To-night there was a dramatic turn in the situation when President Farrell asked his friend Colonel Peron to take over the Government. Colonel Peron, who is in a military hospital with pleurisy, refused, but demanded the immediate resignations of the two men who overthrew him— General Avalos and Admiral Vernengo Lima. Both these men have left Government House, and the impression is that they have resigned.

In Avellaneda, it is said that 40,000 meat workers and 5,000 railwaymen are striking, while the glass and textile workers are also out. Trains are running irregularly, if at all, and travelling is dangerous owing to the possibility of sabotage. In many neighbouring towns and villages the shops have closed owing to the ferment. The tumult in Buenos Aires is such that it seems that only Colonel Peron or a thunderstorm could calm the people.

The police have announced that Colonel Peron arrived at the central military hospital here early to-day in a heavily guarded motor-car, and his triumph as hero of the Argentine workers gained fresh impetus when four workmen delegates, accompanied by President Farrell's aide-de-camp, were allowed to go to the hospital, where they greeted him on behalf of the people.

"LONG LIVE THE POLICE"

Among the slogans heard in Buenos Aires streets during the past 24 hours were: " Peron, Peron, and nobody else " ; " One million votes for Peron " ; " To the gallows with the bourgeoisie " ; " Long live Velazco " (ex-police chief) ; and " Long live the police."

It is stated that when a strong force of police encountered a column of marching workers, a police officer approached the demonstrators and asked them to disperse because " otherwise they would place the police in an embarrassing position."

Eye-witnesses were astonished at the extraordinarily cordial relations which were apparent between the factory workers and the police, contrasting with the bitter hatred shown on other occasions when the police clashed with well-dressed crowds. From this, it is presumed, the police sympathize with Colonel Peron.

The Argentine General Confederation of Labour has called a 24-hour strike for Colonel Peron for to-morrow. To-day trains on the British-owned Buenos Aires Great Southern Railway were prevented from running by the railwaymen, who placed themselves on the track against the trains. In other parts signals were cut and rails torn up.

The British Ambassador, Sir David Kelly, to-day visited the Minister of Marine, Admiral Vernengo Lima, who is acting Foreign Minister, to ask that everything possible be done to protect the British-owned Argentine railways against sabotage in to-morrow's announced general strike. The acting Foreign Minister promised to do his best. Sir David Kelly had difficulty in approaching Government House through the surging mass of workers, but when the Union Jack on his car was recognized there were cries of " Viva Inglaterra," and the people made way.

CABINET RESIGNATION

BUENOS AIRES, Oct. 17. President Farrell announced to-night that the Argentine Cabinet had resigned. He made this statement while addressing a crowd that had gathered outside Government House, in the Plaza del Mayo. He added that the Government would not be handed over to the Supreme Court.—Reuter

THE ARGENTINE CONTEST

◆

CULMINATION OF A VIOLENT ELECTION CAMPAIGN

CHOICE BETWEEN PERÓN AND TAMBORINI

From a Correspondent lately in Argentina

After two and three-quarter years of *de facto* military government the Argentine people will go to the polls to-morrow to elect a new President and Vice-President, and simultaneously to choose a federal Congress and renew all the provincial authorities and legislatures throughout the country. Never before in modern times has an Argentine Presidential election been held in such an atmosphere of turbulence and violence.

During the past six months fights between political factions and shooting in the streets have become a regular feature of Buenos Aires night life. Sometimes three or four separate shooting affrays occur on one evening. The smarting pain of tear gas is now familiar to the eyes of Buenos Aires citizens. Crowds have been seen after the departure of the police to light fires in the street to disperse the gas.

In to-morrow's Presidential election here are two candidates. One is the well-loved and well-hated dynamic, dashing, picturesque, colourful, and often reckless Colonel Juan Domingo Perón, Argentina's most vivid personality since the death 13 years ago of the famous old Radical, President Hipólito Irigoyen. Colonel Perón's opponent is Dr. José P. Tamborini, of Italian descent and a physician by profession, who until his proclamation as the Radical candidate was almost unknown by sight to the great majority of Argentines, although he had been Minister of the Interior under President Marcelo de Alvear from 1925 to 1928. President Farrell promised seven months ago that, contrary to precedent, in this election there would be no " official " candidate.

PARTY INTERESTS

Nevertheless, Colonel Perón is the nearest approach to an official candidate that could be imagined. In Argentina a " Caudillo," or leader with a personal following, is more important than a party or programme. The Labour Party and the Peronista Radical Party have been created for the express purpose of sponsoring Colonel Perón's candidature. The Labour Party is by far the more important and represents a great but undetermined number of clerks, workers, and peons who benefited from Perón's social reforms while he was Secretary of Labour and Welfare.

The Peronista Radicals are a small group who broke away from the great but disunited Radical Party attracted by Perón's magnetism and the conviction that his star was ascending. It has been said that Argentine Radicalism is not a party but an " attitude of mind." The Argentine Nationalists, who are more conspicuous for their quality than quantity, have resolved to support Perón ; but the Labour Party has, perhaps wisely, repudiated any association with the Nationalists on account of the latter's totalitarian leanings. Colonel Perón also enjoys the support of part of the Army and the wholehearted allegiance of a large and well-trained police force, who regard Perón as a demi-god and constitute a veritable Pretorian Guard.

Dr. Tamborini represents not only his own party, the Radicals, but also the other parties in the Coalition or Democratic

Union comprising Socialists, Communists, and Progressive Democrats (a small party strong only in the Province of Santa Fé). Furthermore Tamborini will receive the votes of the Conservatives, traditional enemies of the Radicals. The Conservatives, while contesting the Congressional election as a party, have decided not to proclaim a Presidential candidate.

PERÓN'S OPPONENTS

Dr. Tamborini has none of Colonel Perón's glamour and mystic appeal, but he is the spokesman for all those who hate Colonel Perón, ranging from wealthy landowners and captains of industry to the workmen's leaders and left-wing agitators whom Colonel Perón once imprisoned in the bleak wastes of Patagonia. Included among Perón's opponents are many members of the Argentine middle class and whatever following the former Labour leaders, dismissed by Perón, still have among the workers.

Almost the whole Argentine property-owning class supports Dr. Tamborini, not for his own merits but because he opposes Colonel Perón. Big industrialists who support Colonel Perón can be counted on the fingers of one hand. The Argentine Navy, although scarcely a political factor, is resolutely opposed to Perón because it believes that soldiers should serve and not rule. The only outstanding naval officer on Perón's side is Rear-Admiral Alberto Teisaire, former Minister of Marine.

The Catholic Church in Argentina is capable of playing a leading part in any political election and is too important to be overlooked. Its influence has not been thrown decisively on either side, but it veers definitely towards Colonel Perón, owing to the Church's disapproval of Socialists and Communists and because the Radicals have included the principle of lay teaching in their programme. Colonel Perón, however, by no means enjoys unqualified ecclesiastical approval. Paradoxically, both sides in the present contest profess championship of democracy and both invoke the magic name of the great Radical, Hipólito Irigoyen.

The leading figures in the Democratic Union and among its associates of the Conservative Party are mostly elderly men who have been prominent in Argentine public life for 30 years or more. The stalwarts of Perón's Labour Party, on the other hand, are unknown persons, mostly insignificant and of humble origin. Of members of the old political parties who entered Perón's camp, three are fairly known Radicals. These are Dr. Cooke, Minister of Foreign Hortensio Quijano, Vice-Presidency; do Antille. tained

only two recruits—Dr. Juan Atil Bramuglia, until recently Governor Buenos Aires Province, and Señor Ang Borlenghi, leader of the Federation Commercial Employees.

Colonel Perón's closest personal a political associates are his former milita colleagues—Colonel Domingo A. Me cante, who succeeded Perón as Secreta of Labour and Welfare and is regarde as Perón's shadow; General J. Filome Velazco, Chief of Police (Colonel Peró midnight visits to police headquarte have often been cause for conjecture and, of course, Rear-Admiral Teisaire.

An Argentine military Revolutiona Government inevitably looks with sor dismay at the prospect of handing ov power to a civil democratic administr tion, owing to fear of wholesale repris against those who overthrew the Consti tion. Hence many Argentine milita officers would prefer to see Perón elect President for six years with a Congre After that period civil democracy cou be restored without fear of retributio and vengeance. This solution was tri after the right-wing revolution of 19 which was led by Lieut.-General J Félix Uriburu. General Agustin P. Jus became President in a comprom administration, and his successor, civilian, Dr. Roberto M. Ortíz, w rapidly restoring democracy in Argenti when he died.

GUARDING AGAINST FRAU

Fears have been expressed by democratic Opposition that the conduct to-morrow's election may not be abo suspicion in spite of the promise of Minister of the Interior, General Fel Urdapilleta, that the election would "free, fair, and crystal-clear." T Government's decision that the Arm Navy, and Air Force, instead of the poli shall guard the ballot-boxes has not be sufficient to allay all anxiety. Since t passing, in 1912, of the Sáenz Peña L which made voting free, secret, a obligatory, all Argentine Presidential el tions have been accompanied by so degree of violence. The elections of 19 and 1937, which were "won" by Conservatives and their allies the Ar Personalists, were marked not only violence but also by wholesale fra which consisted in changing the voti papers while the ballot-boxes were their way from the polling-station to counting-house.

It has been said that in Argentina Radical Party, when in power, ne resorted to fraud because they, unl their Conservative opponents, could without it. The federal capital is the o Argentine constituency where it is co sidered impossible for any party to by unfair means. If Colonel Perón should win in the federal capital, as well as in the rest of the country, it would be virtually proof that he had honestly won the election. But the federal capital invariably votes Radical and Socialist with a substantial Conservative minority, and only the blindest of Perón's followers believe that he could win here against the combined Opposition.

Although the possibility of fraud cannot be entirely ruled out, the Opposition fear chiefly wholesale violence. In past elections violence was perpetrated by the police on behalf of the official candidate. When clashes have occurred between the Peronistas and the Democrats, the police have often intervened to protect the Peronistas. In all Argentine history the Opposition have never won a Presidential election against an official candidate, except when the Opposition was led by the great mystic, Hipólito Irigoyen. And yet it was said that no follower of Irigoyen knew why he was an Irigoyenist. In tomorrow's election Colonel Perón is the mystic as well as being almost an " official " candidate.

Argentina at the Polls

To-morrow's presidential election in Argentina has aroused the interest of the entire American world. The assurance of the Argentine Government that " for the " first time for many years the coming " election will be a faithful expression of " the popular will " may be contrasted with the statement of a correspondent whose article appears on this page, that " never before in modern times " has an Argentine presidential election been held in such an atmosphere of turbulence and violence." The political storms centre round the figure of COLONEL JUAN PERÓN, who was a leading member of the military junta which took over power in June, 1943, and has since retained it. Until the resignation last October of his official position and his military rank he was the most important figure in the Government. He now stands for the Presidency as the self-proclaimed champion both of the masses against the piutocracy and of Argentina against the United States.

The election campaign was entering on its final stage when the United States Government published the memorandum on the Argentine situation which it had addressed to the members of the Pan-American Union, a comprehensive indictment based mainly on material discovered in Germany and supported by detailed evidence. No one is more thoroughly implicated in this indictment than COLONEL PERÓN. Some of his alleged offences—his efforts to send an emissary to Germany, and eve.. his activities in organizing a Fascist revolution in Bolivia and in attempting to promote similar movements in Brazil, Chile, Paraguay, and Uruguay — belong to the past. But it is an essential part of the American case that the conditions it describes still prevail. The memorandum submits evidence of a continuing partnership between the military dictatorship and an elaborate Nazi organization in Argentina. It asserts that " the " destruction of organized labour was pro- " jected from the beginning of the military " government," and that the Secretariat of Labour and Social Welfare, of which COLONEL PERÓN was the first head and which he built up on the ruins of the Argentine labour movement, has been used to further his candidature. Quoting a speech · by COLONEL PERÓN himself, it accuses the Argentine Government of aiming at " a thoroughly regimented totali- " tarian State dedicated to the pursuit of a " warlike life and a war economy." It is against this background that COLONEL PERÓN is making his bid for power.

NEW TERM IN ARGENTINA

◆

OPPOSITION TO PRESIDENT PERÓN COLLAPSES

IMPROVED RELATIONS WITH RUSSIA

From Our Buenos Aires Correspondent

Brigadier-General Juan Domingo Perón, who was chosen President of Argentina in the general elections of February 24 last, assumes office to-day, which significantly is the third anniversary of the Argentine military revolution which overthrew the late President Castillo's Conservative oligarchy. Champion of social justice at home and avowed defender of Argentine sovereignty abroad, General Perón is Argentina's twenty-seventh President.

Never before has Argentina known in so short a period such rapid and profound changes in her internal and external situation as those which have occurred in the nine weeks that have elapsed since General Perón's victory became apparent. When the result of the elections was announced, the vast coalition of political parties opposing Perón, comprising Conservatives, Radicals, Progressive Democrats, Socialists, and Communists, after indulging in mutual and bitter recriminations over the causes of its defeat, disintegrated and collapsed. The tremendous campaign of anti-Government agitation, which drew its strength from the property-owning and professional classes, and maintained Argentina in a state of constant turmoil in the second half of last year, ceased suddenly.

The enthusiasm and hopes of the Opposition were based upon the false premise that they enjoyed the support of the overwhelming mass of Argentines, and ⸻n's enemies lost heart when their ⸻ was shattered. The defeated ⸻ the Presidency, Dr. ⸻red that he would ⸻ote given to

General Perón. The Opposition feared only that their followers might be afraid to go to the polls, and, when it became known that the election had been correct and that there had been a record poll they were jubilant. Later, the Socialist organ, La Vanguardia, wrote:—"The lamentable truth is that we have lost an election which we expected to win." Indeed, both sides at first thought that General Perón had lost. The vanquished having sought help from the United States, blamed the United States for their defeat, attributing it especially to the publication of the American Blue Book. Anger and recrimination gave way to a spirit of resignation. Internal peace returned to Argentina, and for the first time for many months the mounted and motorized police disappeared from the streets of Buenos Aires, although the state of siege went on almost unnoticed until it was lifted 10 days ago.

PERONISTAS

Acute dissensions have indeed occurred between the Argentine Labour Party representing the great mass of General Perón's working-class followers, and its erstwhile allies, the Peronista Radicals constituting the upper social strata of the Peronistas. Although the Labour Party is the left wing and the Peronista Radicals are the right wing of Peronismo the schism is more a struggle for the fruits of office than a conflict of ideology. Both wings are blindly devoted to General Perón, whose personality and presidential prerogatives combine to make him omnipotent. The extremely personal character of the new régime is illustrated by General

Perón's appeals to his followers urging that "all Peronistas should stand together."

In foreign affairs, and especially in those relating to the Americas, General Perón's good luck has been scarcely less than in the domestic sphere. Before the elections one of the chief arguments of the Opposition was that Perón's triumph would isolate Argentina in the American Continent. The Peronistas to-day proclaim joyfully that the reverse has occurred and point to the fact that all the Ibero-American nations are sending delegations, composed of their most prominent personages, to attend General Perón's inauguration as President. General Perón has made special efforts to win the friendship of Brazil. Recently, when the new Brazilian Ambassador to Argentina, Dr. Juan Bauptista Lusardo, arrived in Buenos Aires, Perón mobilized his working-class supporters, who met the Ambassador at the railway station carrying Argentine and Brazilian flags and shouting "Perón! Brazil!" General Perón's work and programme of social justice have even won him a certain active support among the proletariat of neighbouring countries. Many Bolivian miners are said to be Peronistas, and mysterious leaflets and posters praising Perón's social policy have appeared in Uruguay.

But the most remarkable change of all in the foreign field has been the great improvement in Argentine relations with Soviet Russia, an occurrence which it is difficult to dissociate from the deterioration in relations between the Soviet Union and the United States. A Soviet trade mission has been in Argentina since April and has not only established personal, if unofficial, contacts with Argentine Ministers and Government departments but has also been received by General Perón himself. And for the first time for more than 15 years four steamers flying the Soviet flag were simultaneously lying in the port of Buenos Aires. Demand for the renewal of Argentine diplomatic relations with Russia, which have been broken since 1917, is coming not only from Argentine Communists but also from many other political sectors, including even the Nationalists who represent the extreme Right.

Some Argentine Nationalists argue that it is merely continuity of foreign policy for Argentina to be friendly with any great Power which is a rival of the United States. Among the names of those who have sponsored a proposal to create an Argentine-Russian Cultural Institute in Buenos Aires there appear several well-known Nationalists who in the past have been notorious anti-Communists. These Nationalists do not wish Argentina to be in Russia's sphere of influence, but merely desire their country to be more independent of the United States. The Nationalists deplored Argentina's declaration of war on Germany and Japan, but have been staunch supporters of General Perón since last October when Perón was overthrown and restored to power. The Nationalists rallied to Perón's side as soon as they realized that the pro-United States elements were against him.

COMMUNIST SUPPORT

The Argentine Communists have displayed a spirit of reciprocity towards those who are well disposed towards Russia, and many Argentine observers believe that the day is imminent when the Communists will support General Perón openly. Such an event would have seemed impossible a few months ago, when the Communists were denouncing Perón as a Nazi and a Fascist. The official organ of the Argentine Communist Party, *La Hora,* is in fact already championing the cause of Perón's Labour Party in its internal quarrel with the Peronista Radicals, and is urging that all Argentine workers should unite irrespective of whether they are Peronistas or not.

Less than a year ago General Perón was reported to have said that he would not cease persecuting the Communists until he had reached an agreement with them. Since then, Perón has emancipated the Communists and defeated them in a fair election. Communist emancipation benefited Perón more than the Communists, because the Communists entered the Opposition or "democratic" camp and Perón was thus given the Catholic vote, which was incomparably bigger than the Communist vote. The Argentine Communists are negligible as a factor in themselves, but are important as a link with Soviet Russia. Many Peronistas believe that friendship with the Soviet would help General Perón both morally and materially—by allaying lurking suspicions that General Perón had a semi-Fascist past and by enabling Argentina to play Russia against the United States. Most Peronistas would infinitely prefer Argentina's old friend, Great Britain, to play this role, but fear that there is no hope of it happening.

THE ARMS EMBARGO

The refusal of the United States to supply arms to Argentina, and the consent of Great Britain and Sweden to follow the United States in this matter are undoubtedly driving Argentina towards Moscow. This express refusal to supply arms is regarded by wide sectors of Argentine public opinion as discriminatory, mortifying, and wounding to Argentine pride. How different it would be, they say, if Argentina maintained cordial relations with Russia! For this reason, Argentine Nationalists and Communists, the two extremes which are diametrically opposed ideologically, to-day are beginning to talk with a common voice.

The Argentine Foreign Minister, Dr. Juan Cooke, has more than once recently expressed the hope that the visit of the Soviet trade mission will lead to diplomatic relations between Argentina and Russia, and messages from Moscow suggest that this view is reciprocated. Argentines argue that friendship with Russia need not cause bad relations with the United States, but, on the contrary, might even improve Argentine-United States relations. In any case, Argentina might find herself in a better bargaining position.

Excessive friendship with Moscow, however, would not entirely suit General Perón's internal position, since it might bring him the disapproval of the Catholic Church, without whose benevolence General Perón could hardly have been elected President of Argentina. The Buenos Aires daily newspaper *El Pueblo*, the chief organ of Argentine Catholic opinion, has already published an editorial deploring any idea of relations with Russia.

HOLIDAY MOOD IN BUENOS AIRES

WORKERS ACCLAIM GEN. PERÓN

From Our Own Correspondent

BUENOS AIRES, AUG. 22

Soon after daybreak to-day processions of workers from all parts of Argentina carrying banners with the slogan "Juan Perón Eva Perón 1952-1958" began arriving in the Avenida Nueve de Julio, reputed to be the world's widest avenue, in readiness for the afternoon demonstration organized by the Government-sponsored General Confederation of Labour. The demonstrators came to ask General Perón and his wife to accept candidature for the presidency and vice-presidency in the elections fixed to take place on November 11, which will determine who shall rule Argentina during the next six years.

All non-essential activities were suspended by the General Confederation of Labour, which ordered a general stoppage of work. Flags flew from almost every building, including such Opposition strongholds as the offices of the newspaper *La Nacion,*, the Argentine Rural Society, and the Jockey Club, in these cases prudence evidently taking precedence over conviction. Indeed, any open display of opposition in Buenos Aires to-day would have been inviting trouble. Although General Perón and Señora Perón are undoubtedly popular among the poorer classes, to-day's demonstration was a masterpiece of organized enthusiasm. Visitors from the provinces, mostly poor workers, were given free food and travel.

After midnight to-night theatres, cinemas, and even the opera house in Buenos Aires will be open to provincial visitors free as guests of the General Confederation of Labour. After midday the bankrupt Buenos Aires city transport corporation allowed all passengers to travel without tickets on tramcars, omnibuses, and underground railways.

ARMY DISAPPROVAL

Although it is winter in Argentina, the day broke sunny and warm—" Perón's weather," Peronistas say, because Peronista demonstrations have always been favoured with fine weather.

General Perón took his place on the platform in the Avenida Nueve de Julio about 5 o'clock and Señora Perón came 15 minutes later. There was a speech by Señor Jose Espejo, leader of the General Confederation of Labour, while squadrons of civil aircraft flew overhead. Military aircraft did not take part because the demonstration was regarded as a spontaneous gesture by workers.

General Perón and Señora Perón both addressed the gathering and said, regarding the candidatures, that they would accept whatever decision the people imposed. Thereupon Señor Espejo said the demonstration would adjourn and continue to-morrow. Señora Perón then spoke again and asked the people to give her four days for a definite decision on acceptance or refusal of the Vice-Presidency. Señor Espejo said the people wanted an immediate decision and the General Confederation of Labour would call a general strike if Señora Perón did not accede. She finally promised to give a decision later to-night.

The General Confederation of Labour estimated to-day's crowd at 1,500,000, but private estimates are about 300,000.

To-day's gathering aroused more inquisitive interest than other Peronista demonstrations. Both candidates had indicated that they would bow to the people's will. While the General Confederation of Labour has sponsored Señora Perón's candidature, the Army is understood to disapprove mainly because she is a woman and very dominant. Señora Perón said significantly at a recent Army, Navy, and Air Force dinner party that the present Argentine régime counted more on the support of the workers than on the Army.

It is reported that General Perón contemplates visiting Brazil after his re-election as President, the possibilities of an electoral defeat being considered negligible. During his absence Señora Perón, if elected Vice-President, would automatically become acting President and Commander-in-Chief of the armed services—an extraordinary and unprecedented event in Argentina.

The Council of the Peronista Party to-night announced that it had formally nominated General Perón as candidate for the Presidency and Señora Perón as candidate for the Vice-Presidency. To-morrow has been decreed a public holiday throughout Argentina.

Upset in Argentina

When GENERAL PERÓN and his wife were invited a fortnight ago to stand for the Presidency and Vice-Presidency, most people took their joint election for granted. The invitation could not have been more public or more elaborately prepared. Work was officially suspended throughout Argentina; railway tickets to Buenos Aires were free for all; all the apparatus of the Government trade unions was employed to bring huge numbers to the capital to support the two Perón candidatures. It is even reported that the arrangements for feeding the crowds gave the final blow to any hopes of keeping up shipments of meat to Britain in the second half of August; meat-eating is a serious business in Argentina.

The Government party chose to make an unprecedented fuss about the candidatures, and in the outcome it has suffered a resounding setback. Some of the Army leaders had not concealed their lack of enthusiasm at the thought of a woman Vice-President acting as President and Commander-in-Chief in the events of her husband's absence abroad, illness, or death. SEÑORA PERÓN has shown herself a forceful personality and a politician to be taken seriously; her hold on Argentinian labour rests on something more than her flamboyant manner and is by no means unreal. In her husband's movement she is publicly the champion of social change; her appeal to Argentinian labour, emotionally expressed, is a left-wing appeal. This fact may have heightened the Army's opposition, though the fact that she is a woman would be enough.

These military feelings were taken to explain the demonstration organized by the Government on August 22; an overwhelming display of mass sentiment was to remind the Army that it was not the master. The plan went awry. It had the opposite effect. European democracies would consider a crowd of about 300,000 large enough, but two million demonstrators had been ordered and the General Confederation of Labour failed to assemble them. In the broad avenues of Buenos Aires the deficiency was marked. An embarrassing delay followed, in which it slowly became clear that all had not gone well; finally SEÑORA PERÓN announced in a broadcast marked by all her familiar charm that she had decided not to stand.

The GENERAL's candidature will go forward, and there is no reasonable doubt that he will be elected to a second term as President; indeed, there has been no suggestion that he has any rival for the leadership of Argentina. Yet the incident has important implications. It suggests either an unexpected weakness of organization in the Government party or, more probably, a division; few people believe that the Peronista machine could not have brought in its two million people if it had set out whole-heartedly to do so. It seems inevitable that there should now be a party inquest, beginning with the General Confederation of Labour, which can hardly escape responsibility.

The chain of events by which GENERAL PERÓN and his wife turned a precarious position in an unstable political system into a massive radical dictatorship on a new model has a fascination of its own; but it is always permissible to speculate on the point at which, as has invariably happened in Latin America and usually in other countries, the mass appeal falters and the demagogic force begins to disperse. GENERAL PERÓN may not yet have cause for qualms, but he and SEÑORA PERÓN, and their party, have for the first time been obliged to renounce an intention publicly formed. He has had an uncomfortable reminder of the traditional role played by the Army in South American politics. The Army has been silent since 1945, when it tried to overthrow him and failed. Now, for the first time since then, it has asserted its wishes and the PRESIDENT has had to accept them.

PRESIDENT PERÓN AND FOREIGN INTERESTS

READY TO "TEACH A LESSON"

BUENOS AIRES, June 8.—President Perón, addressing sugar workers at Government House to-day, said: " I cast out of the country all big foreign interests. I bought everything they had, though I never paid them one centavo. That is why I have become public enemy No. 1 of the imperialist concerns—people who took millions away from us and now cannot do it; people who got our meat free and now must pay for it."

He added that he was ready to teach a lesson to all his foreign enemies, who, he alleged, financed his political opponents. He did not care whether all the newspapers of the world were against him. " If they like to think they an attack, let them try. We shall only reply once, but in such a way that neither they nor their children will ever come again. They will not have a chance to think of it."

Señora Eva Perón, wife of the President, will advance more than 3m. pesos (about £75,000) to pay two months' wages (April and May) due to 1,700 employees of the successor to the independent newspaper *La Prensa*, which the Government took over in April. An official statement to-day said that the newspaper's representatives had " systematically opposed all suggestions."—*Reuter.*

100,000 CHILDREN SUPPORT GEN. PERÓN

FREE TOYS AND CAKES

FROM OUR OWN CORRESPONDENT

BUENOS AIRES, AUG. 17

A new note in General Perón's propaganda was struck to-day when a crowd of Argentine children estimated at 100,000 accompanied by their parents assembled in and around Luna Park stadium here to ask General Perón and señora de Perón to stand as candidates for the Presidency and Vice-Presidency of Argentina in the November elections. The stadium was quickly filled and overflow meetings were held outside. Thousands of toys were given to the children while motor-vans distributed fruit and cakes.

ARGENTINE "LOYALTY" CELEBRATIONS

PARADE OF ARMED FORCES

FROM OUR OWN CORRESPONDENT

BUENOS AIRES, OCT. 17

Argentine workers to-day celebrated the " Day of Loyalty," the anniversary of General Perón's triumph six years ago when he returned from his imprisonment in the island fortress of Martin Garcia. This year's celebrations aroused special interest because for the first time the Army took part in what has hitherto been regarded exclusively as the workers' day of rejoicing. The Government evidently wishes, in view of the recent military rising and the forthcoming elections, to identify the armed forces with the workers' cause.

A parade comprising all branches of the Argentine armed forces was held this morning and was attended by General Perón, while squadrons of aircraft flew overhead.

General Perón and Señora Perón and leaders of the General Confederation of Labour appeared on the balcony of Government House this evening. General Perón conferred on his wife the Grand Peronista Medal of loyalty as a reward for resigning her candidature for the vice-presidency in the coming elections. Señor Espejo, leader of the Confederation of Labour, then decorated her with the " Laurels of Recognition " on behalf of the Confederation. Señora Perón made a short speech, but was so weak that she was unable to stand without help.

At the end of the ceremony General Perón announced that to-morrow would be a public holiday—" Saint Evitas Day." His wife's christian name is Eva or Evita.

TWO CHURCH LEADERS EXILED BY ARGENTINA

◆

RAIDS ON ROMAN CATHOLICS: JUDGE IMPEACHED

FROM OUR OWN CORRESPONDENT

BUENOS AIRES, Wednesday.

The Peron régime to-day sent into exile two Roman Catholic Church leaders as " instigators " of the outbreak of violence last week-end, when supporters of the Government's anti-Church campaign clashed with Roman Catholics.

The régime has also started impeachment proceedings against a Supreme Court judge who suggested that Roman Catholics were not guilty of provoking disturbances. Before dawn police raided, and in many cases closed, parochial offices and headquarters of the lay Catholic Action organisation throughout the country.

In these sorties the police were seeking evidence to support their charges against the Church.

The expelled Church dignitaries are Mgr. Manuel Tato, Auxiliary Bishop of Buenos Aires, and his assistant, Mgr Ramon Novoa. Mgr. Tato has been acting as head of the Church in Argentina during the illness of the Primate, Cardinal Copello.

While police with 20 machine-guns stood by at the airport the two men were placed aboard a State airlines plane for Rome.

Although both are Argentinian citizens, they were flown out because of "allegiance to a foreign flag." They were dismissed from Federal posts by decree yesterday, and a few hours later were taken to central police headquarters for interrogation.

CATHEDRAL CLASH

Judge " Interfered "

The Church has denied responsibility for disorders in which the Argentine flag was burned and an arson attempt was made at the Cathedral. It has been supported by Judge Tomas Casares, of the Supreme Court, who was in the Cathedral during the attack.

A Government Bill of impeachment sent to Congress for immediate action alleged that he attempted to interfere with police investigation, and on his own authority requested military protection for the Cathedral and the 500 inside.

The situation continues to be tense. More windows were broken in the main shopping centre during the night, when workers burnt the effigy of a priest.

NOT ALLOWED LUGGAGE

DETAINED OVERNIGHT

RIO DE JANEIRO, Wednesday.

On arrival here to-day in an airliner bound for Rome Mgr. Tato and Mgr. Novoa said they had been put in the plane by Argentine police after being held in prison since yesterday.

They said they were not allowed to take any belongings. Mgr. Tato said : " In spite of being Argentines, we were expelled to Rome, and with only the clothes on our backs."

A member of the airliner's crew said they had been told the men were being deported as " dangerous Italian characters." Mgr Tato commented : " Nonsense. We are not Italians and we are not dangerous. We both were born in Argentina."—B.U.P.

BISHOP DENIES DISRESPECT TO PERON REGIME

HELD 12 HOURS

FROM OUR OWN CORRESPONDENT
LISBON, Thursday.

Mgr. Tato, Auxiliary Bishop of Buenos Aires, and Mgr. Ramon Novoa, Canon of the diocese, who were expelled from Argentina by the Peron Government after being arrested, reached Lisbon to-day on their way by air to Rome.

At the Airport Mgr. Tato said he could find no explanation for the arrests. They were made without a charge being brought.

He denied that disrespect had been shown the Argentine flag by Roman Catholics during the Corpus Christi procession in Buenos Aires as was alleged by the Peron authorities "No Roman Catholic would do such a thing."

"By order of the Bishops the national flag was always displayed by the altar in Argentine churches."

CAPTAIN HAD PASSPORTS

He said that after being held incommunicado for 12 hours he and Mgr. Novoa were taken to the airport. They had only the clothes they were wearing. The captain of the plane had their passports and had instructions to hand them to the Italian police.

"Our departure was spectacular. We were taken to the plane by quite an escort. 10 coach-loads of men carrying machine-guns."

Mgr. Tato said there was no logical reason for the present anti-Church campaign in Argentina. Before the campaign President Peron had always shown himself to be a Roman Catholic. The country's constitution ruled that the President must be Roman Catholic.

Driven to Vatican

Our Rome Correspondent telephoned last night:

Mgr. Tato and Mgr. Novoa arrived in Rome to-night after a stop in Madrid. They were met at the airport by the Pro. Secretary of State, Mgr. Tardini, and by the president of the Italian Catholic Action, Dr. Gedda. Busloads of Catholic Action youths and priests of the Argentine College in Rome were present.

The two prelates were driven immediately to the Vatican. It was reported that they will be received by the Pope to-night, as he is anxious to have first-hand information of the situation in Argentina.

VATICAN BAN ON ARGENTINE GOVERNMENT

DECREE ISSUED

FROM OUR OWN CORRESPONDENT
ROME, Thursday.

The Holy See to-day excommunicated all those in Argentina who have "trampled upon the rights of the Church" and "used violence against Church personalities."

The Consistorial Congregation of the Vatican did not name President Peron—in the case of persecution of the church excommunication is always collective. But there was no doubt that the President and his Government fell under the penalty, which excludes a Roman Catholic from communion. The decree said:

Since in the Argentine Republic the rights of the Church have recently been trampled upon and violence has been used against Church personalities,

Since recently some people have not only dared lay hands on the person of the most excellent Manuel Tato, titular Bishop of Aulon, Auxiliary and Vicar-General of Buenos Aires archdiocese, but have impeded him in the exercise of his jurisdiction and have expelled him from Argentine territory,

The Consistorial Congregation declares and admonishes that all those who have committed such offences—principals of all kinds and grades, the necessary accomplices and those who caused the offences to be committed and which would not have been committed without their participation—have incurred the excommunication "latae sententiae" specially reserved to the Holy See in accordance with Canon Law.

PRESIDENT'S POSITION

In Vatican circles a "vitandi" excommunication against President Peron for heresy is not considered impossible. This would oblige all Roman Catholics to break off religious and civil communication with him.

The persecution of the Roman Catholic Church in Argentina is considered in many ways graver even than that carried out in Eastern Europe. It is said that had Cardinal Mindszenty and Cardinal Stepinac agreed to leave Hungary and Jugoslavia they would not have been imprisoned

NEW BROADCAST BY GEN. PERON

ELECTION PLEDGE ON CHURCH ISSUE

---

202 KILLED, 964 HURT IN BUENOS AIRES

CONTINUED REBEL ACTIVITY REPORTED IN PROVINCES

For the second time in 24 hours President Peron broadcast to the people of Argentina yesterday, assuring them that the revolt by the Navy was over. He promised that the issue of the separation of the Roman Catholic Church from the State would be settled through the forthcoming general election.

Señor Luis Cornes has been appointed Navy Minister, replacing Rear-Adml. Olivieri, who is said to have disappeared after the rebellion. Buenos Aires casualty lists compiled by the General Confederation of Labour put the dead at 202 and wounded at 964.

Reports from outside Argentina said that the rebels were still active in the provinces, and that Rosario, the country's second city, was in their hands. This was denied in Buenos Aires.

The two Roman Catholic churchmen who were expelled by Gen. Peron were received in audience by the Pope. In Washington Dr. Cesar Bunge, economic counsellor to the Argentine Embassy, resigned in protest at the Peron régime.

PILLAGE "BY COMMUNISTS"

FROM OUR SPECIAL CORRESPONDENT

NEW YORK, Friday.

Argentine was in a state of siege to-day as President Peron called on Congress to declare martial law. He spoke on the radio for 13 minutes, his second broadcast in 24 hours.

He said that justice would be meted out to all those who took part in yesterday's abortive rebellion. But justice "would be under the law."

"I am a Catholic and we have many Catholics with us," he said. "We are not attacking religion.

"Let us not try to decide things with violence, but by popular vote." He insisted that the people await the outcome of forthcoming elections for a constituent Assembly to decide if the Roman Catholic Church and State were to be separated.

ARMY STOOD FIRM
Reason For Failure

He repeated yesterday's assertion that the rebellion failed because the Army had stood firm. He also renewed his charge that Roman Catholic priests were partly responsible for the rebellion, which was organised by youthful Navy and Air Force officers.

He gave an assurance, however, that the Government would not allow further attacks on churches. The Communists, he declared, had taken advantage of the confusion to set fire to churches. This charge followed a Government announcement that Communists had committed acts of pillage.

Reports reaching New York from Montevideo state that Peronist demonstrators fired six churches and one basilica in the heart of Buenos Aires where the heaviest fighting took place. They also state that the palace of Cardinal Copello was set on fire but that the prelate, who is 75, was not there at the time.

In Cordoba crowds burned down the headquarters of the Opposition Radical party, tore up a fence round St. Dominic's Church and stoned other targets.

Casualty reports vary, but the General Confederation of Labour gave the total as 202 dead, 964 wounded, based on hospital lists. One Buenos Aires paper puts the dead at 360.

NAVY v. ARMY
Battle in the City

One of the first despatches from Buenos Aires after the reopening of communications said that naval planes flew over the capital between 1 p.m. and 5 p.m., dropping bombs and machine-gunning Government House, the Treasury Ministry, the headquarters of the General Confederation of Labour and other buildings.

Rebel Glenn Martin and Catalina planes were reported to have come from Punta del Indio naval base at the mouth of the River Plate, 100 miles from the city. One Air Force Gloster Meteor joined the rebel forces.

As soon as the first bomb fell, firing broke out between naval forces in the Ministry of Marine building and loyal Army forces in Government House and the Army building—a few hundred yards from each other. Fighting also broke out between rebel marines in the port area and soldiers.

The Ministry of Marine building ran up a white flag after an hour and a half, and all inside were taken prisoner. Marines in the port zone were overpowered by loyal troops.

BOMB IN STREET
Gen. Peron's Escape

Gen. Peron narrowly escaped death from one of the bombs, it was reported. He left the balcony of the Army building just before a bomb fell in the street in front of the balcony.

A general strike called by the Peronist General Confederation of Labour paralysed Buenos Aires to-day. It was called in mourning for yesterday's loss of life.

The port of Buenos Aires across the River Plate from Montevideo is closed to shipping. All air traffic has been suspended.

An unidentified radio station claiming to be the clandestine organ of the rebel command said to-day that two Argentine warships assumed to be the cruisers 25 de Mayo, 6,800 tons, and the Pueyrredon, 6,100 tons, joined the naval base at Puerto Belgrano, in the southern Buenos Aires Province.

It was from Puerto Belgrano, the broadcast claimed, that the Navy forces had revolted. The fleet was concentrated there under Rear-Adml. A. Olivieri, who was Navy Minister until yesterday. He has been replaced by Senor Luis Cornes.

The clandestine station said that the Army garrisons of Corrientes and Entre Rios provinces, and the cities of Rosario and Cordoba, arose against the Government.

Other reports said that the revolt was still "in full swing" in the provinces and that Rosario, which is Argentina's second city, with a population of 500,000, was still in rebel hands.

This was denied by the newspaper La Prensa, which said that Rosario was not, and had not been, in the hands of rebel forces. A group which broke into the radio station there, it said, had fled after making a proclamation.

GEN. PERON SAID TO BE OUSTED

"NOW PRESIDENT IN NAME ONLY"

ARMY JUNTA RULING UNDER GEN. LUCERO

REPEAL OF ANTI-CHURCH LAWS REPORTED

All the signs in Buenos Aires point to the "virtual disappearance" of President Peron from the political scene in Argentina, according to a despatch which reached Reuters in London at midnight. The message had been telephoned from Buenos Aires to another South American capital.

The current feeling in the Argentine capital, the despatch said, is that Gen. Peron is President in name only, and that the country's affairs are in the hands of the military junta headed by Gen. Lucero.

As reported in THE DAILY TELEGRAPH yesterday, Gen. Lucero has been appointed C.-in-C. of the "Forces of Repression." The military are now said to be discussing the President's future.

In a telephone conversation with the newspaper Toronto Telegram Mr. F. Charpentier, Canadian Chargé d'Affaires in Montevideo, Uruguay, said it was apparent that Gen. Peron had been ousted from office. He reported that the new Administration had repealed all the President's anti-Roman Catholic laws.

LONDON, TUESDAY, JUNE 21, 19

He also said he had heard that Gen. Lucero's "compromise" Government had proclaimed an amnesty releasing most of the imprisoned rebels, including 160 Navy men arrested on Thursday after the bombing of the capital.

"*It is* apparent that, for the moment, the rebellion is over and that Peron is not the country's leader any more," he added. "It is a military regime under Gen. Lucero."

NAME OMITTED
Press Silence

According to Reuter, for the first time in 10 years Gen. Peron's name has practically disappeared from the newspapers. Only Democracia made a mention of him spending Sunday in the Presidential Palace 10 miles from the city.

His whereabout are not known. He did not attend the oath-taking in the ceremony yesterday in the Plaza de Mayo marking Argentina's "Day of the Flag."

Gen. Peron's last appearance was on Saturday. In an address to union executives at the headquarters of the General Confederation of Labour he then said that he believed he represented "the will of the Argentine people."

But he added: "I am ready to submit myself to free elections under the control of whoever may want to control them and with absolute freedom for all."

Now 59, Gen. Peron has ruled Argentina for nine years. He was the first constitutionally elected President after a long series of coups d'etat.

CIVIL WAR FEAR
Military Discussions

It is believed the military are doing everything possible to prevent the situation degenerating into a civil war. For this reason they are anxious to keep Gen. Peron as nominal President.

Other reports, however, say discussions are still going on between various Service chiefs, some of whom insist that he must go.

As a result, reports were current in Buenos Aires last evening that Gen. Peron's resignation might be announced at any time, and that all members of his Cabinet have already tendered their resignations.

SPECULATION IN BRAZIL

JUNTA'S POWERS
From EDWIN TETLOW
Daily Telegraph Special Correspondent
RIO DE JANEIRO, Monday.

Links between Argentina and the rest of South America are strengthening, but are still somewhat tenuous and unreliable.

Enough is known to-day in adjoining countries to indicate that comparative peace has returned to Argentina temporarily. It is also clear that a junta, of which President Peron is at least a member, has taken control.

What is not clear from the carefully controlled radio and phone communications is Gen. Peron's exact position after the revolt. Edicts and communiqués are in his name and there is nothing definite to show he is not still in power as dictator.

But in some quarters here there is a feeling that he might have been forced to yield control to two, or possibly three, generals associated with him in the new ruling junta.

Private cable and phone traffic with Buenos Aires has eased considerably within the past 12 hours. Conversations and messages are, however, still being restricted to purely personal or authorised matters.

A hint that the situation within Argentina is not yet restored fully, despite Peronist claims to the contrary, is given in reports that many units of the Army recently engaged in dealing with rebels are still being held at instant readiness.

They are confined to barracks. Their transport and supplies are also being held available for use

Argentina pays tribute to Eva Perón

Buenos Aires, July 26.—General Perón, the former President of Argentina, today made his first official public appearance since his return last month from 18 years in exile when he attended a solemn Mass on the twenty first anniversary of the death of his wife, Eva.

Despite a persistent drizzle crowds of supporters were on hand to cheer him as he arrived at the Buenos Aires cathedral.

Cries of "Perón, Perón", rang out as the general and his third wife Isabel entered the cathedral where Señor Raul Lastiri, the interim President was waiting for them.

Hundreds of uniformed policemen ringed off the main square in front of the cathedral. Plain clothes men were posted on neighbouring buildings.

The police were hard pressed to hold back the crowds who surged forward when General Perón arrived. Some shouted: "Take care of the general."

The former President, who is 77, has been recovering from influenza and heart trouble. Today was only his third outing since he ended his exile on June 20 and took up residence at his home in the suburb of Vicente Lopez.

General Perón and President La_ir_ and their wives occupied a front pew in the packed cathedral.

Also attending was Dr Héctor Cámpora, the former President and General Perón's political protégé, who resigned earlier this month after only seven weeks in office to pave the way for the General's return to the presidency.

After the ceremony, General Perón and his wife left through a side door. But his police motorcycle escort found difficulty in opening a way for his car through the cheering crowds that clustered round it to catch a glimpse of him.

Religious ceremonies were also held throughout Argentina in homage to Señora Eva Perón, who distributed largesse to the poor through her Eva Perón Foundation and died of cancer at the age of 32.

"Evita lives and guides the free fatherland", the pro-Perónist tabloid *Mayoria* said in a headline today.

Newspapers were full of paid advertisements from labour unions and Peronist groups and the city was plastered with posters declaring: "Evita still lives."—Reuter.

Wife takes over reins of power after the death of Gen Perón

From Stuart Stirling
Buenos Aires, July 1

General Juan Domingo Perón died of a heart attack at 1.15pm today in the presidential residence of Olivos in the suburbs of Buenos Aires. He was 78.

His widow, Señora María Estela Perón, who was sworn in on Saturday as interim President, announced his death to the nation in an emotional television speech.

Señora Perón, tears streaming down her face, told her television audience that her husband " gave his life in sacrifice for the peaceful freedom of the Argentine people ".

President Perón, who returned to Argentina last year to win a landslide election after 18 years in exile, was the undisputed leader of the nation and in the past nine months managed to bring a measure of political and economic stability within a democratic system. However, his Government was plagued by the ideological divisions and passions within the Peronist movement and increasing activity by urban guerrillas.

The President's recent middle-of-the-road policies contrasted sharply with his previous affinity for the left, who were responsible for enabling the Peronist candidate, Dr Héctor Cámpora, to win the presidential election last year. This paved the way for General Perón's return from exile.

The general's body will lie in state in the National Congress building in Buenos Aires, although the date for his funeral has not been named. The CGT unions have called a national work stoppage until the burial.

Señora Perón, who becomes the world's youngest President at the age of 43, and the first woman President in the Western hemisphere, has received pledges of support from the trade unions, the armed forces and the Opposition parties, who are united in seeing continuity for the policies of General Perón.

The country's major power groups—the military and right-wing Peronists—are anxious, however, that the Peronist leftists and Marxist guerrillas do not capitalize on the situa-immediate intervention by the military.

Argentina's armed forces will not accept the emergence of the left and they see the new President as capable, even if only temporarily, of continuing the old policies.

Buenos Aires, July 1.—In her broadcast, Señora Perón said the general had fought until his last moments for national unity. She appealed to his friends and opponents to " put aside their personal passions following the death of this great apostle of peace and non-violence ".

The official medical bulletin on his death said he died as a result of heart failure at 1.15 pm. He had been revived after one heart stoppage, but all efforts proved fruitless after the second one.

The Argentine news agency, Noticias Argentinas, reported that the federal police force had put into effect emergency security measures reserved for national crises. Provincial governors were expected to be called soon to the capital.

Señora Perón had been holding her first full-fledged Cabinet meeting when the three doctors attending her husband reported that the end seemed near. The Cabinet meeting quickly broke up as they waited for his death. After the death all radio stations began to play sacred music.

Señora Perón, in her broadcast, said : " I ask friends and adversaries that they calm their personal passions in favour of a free, just and sovereign country . . . I ask that God give me light and strengthen me to fulfil that which God and Perón gave me as a mission."

Tuesday   July 2 1974

PRESIDENT JUAN PERON
Flamboyant creator of modern Argentina

Señor Juan Domingo Perón, whose name dominated the recent history of Argentina, died yesterday at the age of 78. He was President of his country from 1946 to 1955, when he was deposed in a coup d'état, and was called back from exile to be reelected in 1973.

In spite of all the excesses and eccentricities which marked his first period in office, he was undoubtedly one of the most original, talented and versatile leaders ever produced in Latin America. A born leader of men, he had all the qualities needed to appeal to the masses—good looks, personal charm, eloquence, power of oratory, an extraordinary understanding of mass psychology and, what is rare in a dictator, a sense of humour. He created in Argentina a movement that bore his name, whose strength lay in the urbanized working class, which remains the strongest political force in the country.

Few politicians, let alone dictators, even in Latin America have had the experience of being turned violently out of office and then, 18 years later, with all mistakes forgotten, invited back to lead the nation once again. There was a great contrast in his two presidential periods. His great defect which led him to be deposed in 1955 was his inability to rest on his laurels and govern quietly and peacefully. He seemed to be forever seeking new enemies and he thrived on tumult.

During those first nine years his speeches were those of an agitator rather than a ruler, and Argentina acquired increasingly the characteristics of a police state; all forms of freedom allowed to political opponents gradually disappeared. He had the dictator's lonely temperament and most of his early collaborators incurred displeasure and punishment.

He was intolerant of men who showed personality or brilliance and came to be surrounded by insignificant people. After his return from exile in 1973 he basked in his vindication and, now an old man, was content to govern quietly, delegating responsibility to such a degree that it was constantly asked how much control he actually exercised. In fragile health, his main task became one of trying to stop his Peronist movement, which encompassed diverse shades of political opinion, from splitting apart.

Perón was born at Lobos in the Province of Buenos Aires on October 8, 1895, and educated at the International College of Olivos, a suburb of Buenos Aires, and at the International Polytechnic College. He entered the Military College in 1911 and nearly three years later was commissioned lieutenant in an infantry regiment. He was at the Argentine Staff College (Escuela Superior de Guerra) from 1926 until 1929. In all his military examinations he did well without being brilliant. He was professor of military history at the staff college from 1930 until 1936, when he was appointed military attaché in Chile.

He went on a special mission to Italy to study mountain warfare and was greatly impressed by Mussolini. "We shall create a fascism that is careful to avoid all the errors of Mussolini", he was to say later. He wrote a number of books on military operations, including *The Eastern Front in the World War of 1914*, *The Theory of Military History*, *The Russo-Japanese War* in three volumes, and *Operations in 1870* in two volumes, in collaboration with Colonel Enrique Rottjen of the Argentine General staff.

The Argentine military revolution of June 4, 1943, paved the way for Perón's political career. In November, 1943, he was appointed Secretary of Labour and Welfare and began organizing the workers. He was already emerging as the strong man of Argentina, and early in 1944 held simultaneously the three posts of Vice-President, Minister of War, and Secretary of Labour and Welfare. In less than nine months he created his own personal following, and his speeches became steadily more inflammatory. He was still a colonel on October 9, 1945, when military opposition to him came to a head and he was obliged to resign all posts in the Government. Two days later he was arrested and imprisoned in the island fortress of Martín García, in the River Plate.

The political opposition, however, failed to cooperate with the military officers who had overthrown Perón. The Peronists took advantage of their enemies' indecision and spurred on by the oratory of a young actress, Eva Duarte, who was to become his second wife, demonstrated in the streets. Perón was released and addressed the workers from the balcony of Government House on October 17, 1945. He soon announced his intention of standing as candidate for the Presidency in elections fixed for February 24, 1946.

Perón, who by now had been promoted general, won the presidential election with 55 per cent of the votes cast and took office on June 4, 1946. The fairness of this election was not questioned, although there were certain suspicious factors.

After becoming President, Perón accelerated his programme of social reform known as "justicialismo", while his wife, Eva, now idolized by the masses, monopolized the departments of labour and health and dispensed charity through the foundation that bore her name. Perón preached economic emancipation from foreigners, particularly Britain and the United States, and was able to get higher and higher prices for the beef that a war-weary Britain needed. Anglo-Argentine relations reached a low ebb when the British-owned railways were nationalized in 1948.

He was forever putting forward his philosophy of the necessity for Argentina to take a middle way between communism and capitalism and made various bids to make Argentina the leading nation in South America and in the Third World. He was reelected for a second term in November 1951.

Although undoubtedly improving the position of the working classes and accelerating the industrialization of the nation, his economic policies began to prove unsuccessful. By 1952 there were warnings of bankruptcy; and in that year Eva died of cancer.

In April, 1953, while Perón was addressing the workers from the balcony of Government House, two bombs exploded in the Plaza de Mayo, in Buenos Aires, killing six people and wounding 93. The Peronists in reprisal the same night burnt down the Jockey Club of Buenos Aires and the headquarters of the Radical and Socialist parties without interference from the police. A reign of terror followed and about 1,000 people, mostly of the upper class, were arrested.

Even after the first military rising, Perón might have remained President but for two mistakes—his decision to quarrel with the Roman Catholic Church and his grant to an American oil company of a far-reaching and unpopular concession in Southern Patagonia.

His attack on the Church, with whom his relations previously had been cordial, came suddenly in October, 1954, and was precipitated by ecclesiastical disapproval of Perón's personal interest in the organization of girl students. After an initial official press campaign, Perón formally denounced three Argentine bishops by name as "open enemies of the Government". A series of violent measures were rapidly taken against the Church. Anti-clerical street demonstrations were organized by the Government, Roman Catholic processions and ceremonies were banned, divorce was legalized, and a Bill was submitted to Congress to amend the the Constitution and disestablish the Church. The Catholics fought back in defence of their faith, successfully defied police bans, and demonstrated in the streets of Buenos Aires against the anti-religious policy. Rioting occurred almost daily. In the hope of discrediting the Catholics, Perón's Government committed the enormity of burning the Argentine flag and blaming it on the Catholics.

In April, 1955 an agreement was signed between the Argentine Government and the Standard Oil Company of California, whereby the company was to prospect for oil in Patagonia. The concession, which included the right to build airfields, caused such an uproar that even the Peronist Congress failed to ratify it. The armed forces believed that its purpose was to cede military air bases in Argentina to the United States.

A naval and air force rising occurred in and around Buenos Aires on June 16, 1955. Naval aircraft bombed Government House and other strategic points for several hours, while sailors and marines from the Ministry of Marine building attacked Government House by land. The rising failed after about 200 people had been killed and 1,000 wounded. A few hours later the Peronists burnt nine Roman Catholic churches and the archiepiscopal seat in reprisal.

After this second rising Perón was not in complete control of Argentina's destinies, and a third armed rebellion was seen to be only a question of time. He made various efforts to face the gathering storm. He attempted a reconciliation with the Church, sent a telegram to the Pope, appealed for a party truce and promised to rule democratically. When these resorts failed, he made a desperate attempt to save his regime by arming the workers. But it was too late.

On September 16, 1955, simultaneous military, naval, and air force risings occurred in the provinces of Córdoba, Corrientes, Entre Ríos, and Buenos Aires. The Navy was solid in the rebel cause and seized the naval bases of Puerto Belgrano and Río Santiago. Troops and aircraft sent to repress the rebellion changed sides, and after nearly four days' fighting the Peronist generals sued for peace. Perón published an ambiguous letter suggesting that he might withdraw from the scene to facilitate a settlement and avoid further bloodshed and eventually took refuge in a Paraguayan gunboat in Buenos Aires. He went into exile, moving from one republic to another in Latin America; once driven out by a sudden change of government, another time because he had not adhered to the conditions of asylum. Finally, in 1960, Perón, an old friend of General Franco, settled in Spain.

His following in Argentina remained strong and he controlled his party from his opulent home in Madrid. For the next 12 years Peronism—estimated at having the support of about one-third of the nation—bedevilled Argentine politics. The armed forces were anxious to "cleanse the nation of Peronism" and ousted President Frondizi in 1962 when he allowed the Peronists to put forward candidates in the elections.

In 1964 Perón announced to his supporters that he would return to Argentina "within the year". He was to leave his attempted return until December, and some said afterwards that it was only half-heartedly meant. He crossed the South Atlantic, but at Rio de Janeiro the Brazilian authorities turned him back. His dramatic bid to return had fizzled out in humiliation. In Spain the Government demanded stricter assurances from him that he would abstain from political activity. Nevertheless, his third wife, Señora Isabel Martínez de Perón, was active on his behalf—and in January 1966 announced, in Buenos Aires "a high command" of the Peronist movement, dedicated to returning him to power.

The armed forces changed their tactics towards the end of their seven years in power from 1966 to 1973 and General Onganía allowed Perón to make a triumphant return to Buenos Aires in November, 1972. In the first elections of 1973 Perón was unable to stand because of residency requirements imposed by the outgoing military regime, so his close colleague Héctor Cámpora became the standard-bearer for Peronism and was elected with 49 per cent of the vote. He resigned suddenly after only a few months in office and in new elections in September, 61 per cent of the vote went to Perón and his wife, who stood as vice-president.

The majority of Argentinians expected too much. The republic, during this second Peronist age, merely marked time. The fact could not be obscured that the caudillo, despite his broad smile and clear rhetoric, was old and in fragile health. Faced with a dangerous war between the left and right-wings in his movement, he chose the right. The young radicals and guerrilla groups, who had chanted and yelled in the streets for his return in the belief that he would lead them to a new socialist society, were slowly and inevitably becoming disillusioned.

Perón may have died a satisfied man, in his homeland at last and as president once more, but for Argentina it was little more than a short, heady time for nostalgia and illusion.

Appendix II

The legend of *Evita* was born early in Eva Duarte's political career, and gained immortality on July 26, 1952 when she died aged only 32.

Over the next twenty-two years it was nurtured by the macabre odyssey of her specially-preserved corpse. It travelled the globe, beyond the reach of her husband's enemies, the totem of a restless and vibrant faith.

VICEROY'S TALKS IN DELHI TO-DAY

◆

MEETINGS WITH PARTY LEADERS AND PRINCES

BRITISH PLAN TO BE PRES[ENT]OUS

Lord Mountbatten, the V:
Delhi to-day with th-
Ministers rep-
believ-

CALCUTTA ANXIOUS

MUSLIM AND HINDU

MANY INDIANS LIVING

MONDAY JUNE 2 1947

THE TIMES

Is best seen by the way clerks hurry home
for fear
undown
ts
is
nd

DECISIVE PHAS[E]
RELATIONSH[IP]

From Our Own Correspo[ndent]

DELHI

On the eve of to-morrow's [con]-
ference with the Viceroy Indi[a]
turned towards Delhi, where t
leaders are gathered. The cou[n]
with expectancy and the ...g
m! this is in all probabili[ty] ...[g]ed at [l]
at ways, not so much, in order t[o]
[t]as for Hindus & order will be m
e[of] northern l-
'authori[ty]
[s]and
e[r]

THE BRITISH
PRIME MINISTER
STATEMI

[a]nd
[t]he
ill

SEÑORA DE PERÓN TO VISIT LONDON

OR

D

TOUR OF EUROPE

FROM OUR OWN CORRESPONDENT

BUENOS AIRES. JUNE 1

The Argentine President's wife, Doña
Maria Eva Duarte de Perón, who is to
leave for Europe by air on June 6, has
been invited by the British Government to
visit the United Kingdom. The Foreign
Ministry has stated that Señora de Perón
would spend some days in London.

The President's wife was originally invited
by General Franco to visit Spain, and later
it was announced that the tour would include
Rome and the Vatican City, whereupon the
French Government formally invited her to
visit Paris.

The tour has aroused special interest here
because by tradition Argentine Presidents'
wives stay at home, and General Perón's wife
is the first to share her husband's political
activities and public life, overcoming the
barriers and handicaps which affect Argentine
women.

INE 1

l peace
esterday
by the
attended
ding-in-
utenant-
y.   the
ir John

Eva Peron Dies; Fabulous Life Is Ended at 30

Herald Tribune—U.P.
Eva Peron

Argentine Vice-Presidency Almost in Her Grasp: Did Cancer Intervene?

By The United Press

BUENOS AIRES, July 26.—Eva Peron, wife of Argentine President Juan D. Peron, died tonight after a prolonged illness. Her age was given officially as thirty.

The announcement of her death at 8:25 p. m. followed a series of medical bulletins describing her condition as "very serious," "grave" and "declining rapidly." It was announced late today that she had lost consciousness.

[It had been generally understood that she suffered from cancer, although there had been no announcement. She had never fully recovered from an operation performed last November with a New York cancer specialist in attendance.]

She underwent an operation, reportedly for cancer, in November, and her activities diminished. The cause of her illness had not been revealed officially, but it was known that Dr. George T. Pack, a New York cancer specialist, was one of the surgeons.

After the operation, the Argentine first lady made few public appearances. Her last public appearance came on June 4, when she was at her husband's side during his inauguration for a second term. She was very thin, her once photogenic face was shrunken and gray. She did not speak, even when Congressmen stood and cried, "Evita, vice-president," a post she never held.

Cabinet Ministers gathered at the Presidential residence tonight as the increasing urgency of the bulletins indicated that the President's wife lay dying.

A police cordon halted all motor traffic four blocks from the President's home, and pedestrians were allowed to pass only on the other side of the street.

Modern Cinderella

Maria Eva Duarte de Peron, the twentieth-century Cinderella of South America, was one of the most hated and loved, powerful and capricious women in Argentina and the world. Her rise to power was meteoric and her use of that power ruthless in support of her husband's regime. But history may remember her not only as the dictator's wife who crushed democratic institutions to satisfy her personal pique, but also as the ardent feminist who gave Argentine women suffrage and a social worker whose generosity knew no bounds.

Her origins were best forgotten by those who sought favor with the Peron regime. The daughter of Juana Ibarguron, a coachman's daughter, and Juan Duarte, a small landowner who had deserted his legal wife, she was born in the pampas town of Los Toldos, on May 7, 1919—although she later claimed to have been born in 1922—the youngest of their five children born out of wedlock.

The children found small relief from social stigma and snobbery even when, after their father's death, their mother took them to the near-by city of Junin, where she operated a boarding house. At sixteen, after eight years of schooling, Eva left home to travel the 170 miles to Buenos Aires to seek a career on the stage.

Favorite of Military

The next eight years brought personal rather than professional success. Five feet five inches tall, with a well endowed figure, her dark brown eyes and brunette complexion set off by artificially honey-colored hair, Eva Duarte was a favorite with various members of the increasingly powerful military clique.

She was earning 150 pesos a month, about $45, as a minor actress for Radio Belgrano, in 1943, when she met Col. Juan Domingo Peron, then an under secretary in the Ministry of War. As she was seen more frequently in the company of the dark, handsome widower, who subsequently became Vice-President, War Minister and Secretary of Labor and Social Welfare in the government of Edelmiro Farrell, her salary rose to 1,500 pesos and before long she was getting $7,500 a month and roles befitting such a wage.

Installed in a luxurious apartment adjoining that of the politically successful colonel, who was twenty-four years her senior, Eva Duarte was soon the most gossiped-about woman in Buenos Aires. Their mutual success seemed boundless until, in a pre-dawn raid on his apartment, Peron was arrested and forced to resign his government posts. She was immediately dismissed by Radio Belgrano.

Presidential Campaign

Eva Duarte came through this first test of loyalty. She organized a mass demonstration of Peron's supporters, "Los Descamisados," the shirtless ones who were to become her own political province, that turned into a howling riot in front of the federal Government House resulting in Peron's release. A few days later, on Oct. 21, 1945, they were married in a secret civil ceremony in Junin, followed by a public religious ceremony at La Plata on Dec. 10.

Immediately Mrs. Peron set out with her husband on his presidential campaign tour, a thing unheard of for an Argentine woman, and kissed babies—she had none of her own—posed for pictures with peons and distributed gifts like a seasoned politician. When the ballots were counted, she was the First Lady.

Her first acts as First Lady were typical: she banished the nation's leading radio and screen actresses who had snubbed her in her early days; made it illegal for the Ladies of Beneficence, women from the country's oldest and richest families who had scorned her as a social upstart, to continue their charity work, and established the Maria Eva Duarte de Peron Social Aid Foundation which was soon dispensing $12,000 a month to the needy.

Established in the Ministry of Labor, Mrs. Peron showed political keenness and personal drive. She interviewed hundreds of persons a day, from diplomats to dishwashers, spoke at rallies and dedications and soon became the patroness of labor with her strong stand for higher wages and appeal to the masses.

With a $40,000-a-year bill from Paris couturiers alone, a jewel collection reputed to have been exceeded only by Cleopatra's and three rooms of her home serving as storage space for her furs, suits and hats, she nevertheless became the heroine of the poor and needy. She did not hesitate to wear a mink wrap and diamond earrings when addressing her beloved "descamisados," for she would depict herself simply as a shirtless one who had made good in Peron's Paradise, where she and her husband were working to provide such benefits for all.

$4,500,000 a Year

Her foundation, supported on "voluntary" contributions from public employees, labor contracts that provide that workers donate a day's pay each year, and labor unions, provides lavish homes for the aged and for working women in Buenos Aires. On a personal basis she dispensed about $4,500,-000 in charity a year. Soon "Evita," as she urged the workers to call her, was being hailed as "The Madonna of the Humble" and "The Lady of Hope," with her picture—and that of her husband—displayed side by side with religious pictures in the humblest homes of the land.

In 1947 she was invited to Spain by Generalissimo Francisco Franco, who offered her the Order of Isabel la Catolica. In a four-engined plane, accompanied by a lady-in-waiting, a dressmaker, a hairdresser, a physician, secretary and numerous relatives and friends, Mrs. Peron set out on a seventy-eight-day tour that was among the most controversial in political history. It was highlighted by her giving the Falange salute in Spain, having an audience with Pope Pius XII in Rome, being received by the President of France and witnessing the signing of a Franco-Argentine commercial treaty. She was honored at a reception on her way home via Brazil at which the then Secretary of State George C. Marshall proposed a toast to her. But it was also marked by the wolf-whistles of American G. I.s who saw the striking blonde arrive in Italy, left-wing demonstrations in Italy, a shower of stones and over-ripe tomatoes in Switzerland and a complete snub from the British King and Queen, who thwarted her ambition to be a house guest in Buckingham Palace.

The richness of her costumes, her distribution of more than $100,000 to the poor of the countries she visited and her discourses on her feelings for the lower classes brought such caustic comment from the press that "Time" magazine was barred from Argentina for four months because of a cover story on her trip.

She returned nome, however, in a blaze of local glory, to be met by a cheering horde of 100,000, including 10,000 draftees who had been told to doff their uniforms and mingle with the masses to fill out the crowd. She turned her attention to safer ground and won approval for women's suffrage, to be effective in the 1952 elections, with an amendment providing that no woman need reveal her age when she registers.

Her personal business sense was as keen as her political judgments. She was known to control three newspapers, "Democracia," "Laborista" and "Noticias Graficas," to have a registered trademark

Mrs. Peron Dies After Long Illness

Herald Tribune—U.P.

Mrs. Maria Eva Duarte de Peron waving to cheering crowds as she and her husband ride down Buenos Aires' Avenida de Mayo following Mr. Peron's inauguration June 4 for new term as Argentine President. Photograph is one of most recent of Mrs. Peron

under her own name for an agricultural product company and to own an instrument company. She was reported to have purchased a home and established a large bank account in Switzerland, for an eventuality she may have anticipated when she once said, "If I ever go down, watch out for the crash. There won't be anybody else standing up either."

Her personal philosophy which she frequently expressed at public meetings was, "I have three loves —the fatherland, the descamisados and Peron." Apparently the driving force behind her husband, it was said of her that she knew what they both wanted and never let him forget it for long. The role she chose for herself, as she put it to a conference of Argentine governors last year, was, "I try to be a bridge of love and of hope between the people and the leader."

Her brother, Juan Duarte, is secretary to President Peron and thus in a good listening post at the Casa Rosada, or Pink House, where Peron has his offices in downtown Buenos Aires.

Last February, as head of the Peronista Women's party, Mrs. Peron humbly called on her husband, presented him with a watch and urged him to run for re-election to a second six-year term in 1952. It followed logically that in a matter of days there was a boom on for her to run as vice-presidential candidate, in view of women voting for the first time.

A mammoth rally on Aug. 22, attended by 250,000 although planned for 2,000,000, provided the occasion for the government-sponsored General Confederation of Labor to offer the Perons leadership of the ticket for the Nov. 11 elections. They both agreed to bow to the will of the people.

Nine days later Eva Peron, the most politically powerful woman in the Western Hemisphere, declined, in a nation-wide broadcast, the nomination she had maneu-vered to get. She had no higher goal in life, she told the nation, than to serve her country and her husband. "I am not resigning my work," she said, "but just the honors."

It was generally known that her candidacy had caused a split in the command of the Peronist party and that the army was a strong opponent, both because of its displacement in power by the labor unions under her guidance and because of the possibility of a woman becoming President and commander-in-chief. Her husband remained loyal, however, announcing a few days later that "in recognition of her self-denial," in refusing to run, she would be awarded the Grand Peronist Medal, Extraordinary grade.

Paying Last Respects to Eva Peron

President Juan D. Peron (center foreground, back to camera) looks toward coffin as people pay last respects to his wife who lies in state... her funeral tomorrow.

Argentina in Deepest Mourning
Eva Enshrines in Peron's Heart

By The Associated Press

BUENOS AIRES, July 27.—Argentina's First Lady, July 27. Eva Peron today fell to lie in state.

(The United Press reported the body was taken to the Ministry of Labor building where she lay in state until her burial.)

...

ARMY HONOURS FOR MME. PERON

BODY MOVED SECOND TIME IN TWO DAYS

FROM OUR OWN CORRESPONDENT
BUENOS AIRES, Sunday.

With full military honours Mme. Peron's coffin was to-day taken to the headquarters of the General Confederation of Labour. It will remain there for a year until a mausoleum is built in the centre of Buenos Aires and embalming is completed.

The body, which has lain in state at the Ministry of Labour since the day after her death on July 26, was moved to Congress yesterday morning for another day's lying in state.

Before the cortege left to-day 40 lorries carried flowers to the Confederation's headquarters. The ceremonies started with funeral orations. Fifty workers then pulled on the white silk ropes of the gun-carriage and the procession moved off.

The caisson was in the centre of an open square, preceded by police, Gen. José Molina, of the Third Army, and the Military Academy band. It was flanked by nurses of the Fundacion Eva Peron, her private welfare foundation, workers in overalls and Forces' cadets.

PRESIDENT IN PROCESSION

President Peron, relatives, Cabinet Ministers and diplomats walked immediately behind the gun-carriage. The square was closed by eight weapon-carriers and the public fell in behind them.

A 21-gun salute was fired as the cortège reached the Labour headquarters. Lincoln bombers and Meteor jets flew overhead.

Crowds on balconies tossed down flowers as the casket passed, while those in the street bowed.

The nation stopped work to-day under the decree issued by the Confederation of Labour, which joined the Government in inviting the public to watch the procession. Dr. Cesar Iniguez, director of the Cordobas Santarita Hospital, has been dismissed for lack of respect. He failed to observe the mourning period.

Eight die trying to see Eva

BUENOS AIRES, Monday.—
Eight people are reported dead and more than 2,500 hurt in the crush to file past the coffin of Eva Peron.

A former Minister, General Juan Esteban Vacca, died from his injuries in a military hospital. One policeman was killed.

Eva Peron will be buried tomorrow in the Confederation of Labour headquarters with military honours, usually given only to a President who dies in office.

President Peron stood today for half-hour periods at the head of Eva's coffin as the surging thousands pressed forward, weeping and kissing the glass-topped coffin.

Eva crush kills 5

BUENOS AIRES, Tuesday.—
Five people are reported to have been killed, and 100 hurt in the crush at Senora Eva Peron's lying-in-state today. The body is to lie-in-state for a further one or two months.

Senora Peron's last wish was that after her death the poor should write to her and that the Eva Peron Foundation should help them. President Peron has ordered letters to be answered in her name and a pillar-box will be built in the monument to her memory.

Women trampled as they weep for Eva of the two untold secrets

BUENOS AiRES, Sunday. — Weeping women, mourning candles in their hands, were trampled down tonight as thousands struggled to enter the Palace of Labour, where Evita Peron, the radio star who ruled Argentina, lay in state.

Many were hurt in the crush, yet few of the thousands who stood in the rain could answer these two questions:

How old was the President's wife when she died? and
What disease killed her after a fight for life that had lasted ten months?

Her age was given officially as 30. Those who knew her as a child say she was at least 33.

Specialists in many diseases had attended her. Nobody is sure which of them was there to treat her, which as a cover.

In glass coffin

But no doubts on these or other questions affect the grief of the poorer people of Argentina.

For them she will always be the labourer's daughter who became the real ruler of the State.

Two hundred thousand of them lined the two-mile street tonight from the President's palace.

When the body of Eva Peron had been placed in an open coffin covered with glass in the hall of the trade union headquarters, the people filed past 16 ft. away, a stream which will go on for two days.

When the lying-in-state ended, Eva will be buried in t Palace of Labour, where she h her office, to lie there until t planned national monument ready in about two years time.

Tonight President Peron receiv two telegrams.

One was from the Queen. read: "*I extend to you my dee est sympathy and that of r people for the tragic loss whi you and the Argentine people ha sustained in the premature dea of your brilliant and devot partner.*"

Black for life

The other came from Preside Truman — "*Please accept t deepest sympathy of Mrs. Trum and myself in this tragic hour your bereavement.*"

Public demonstrations of gr and mourning are to be bigg than anything before known Argentina—or anywhere else.

Members of the Peron Par have been ordered to wear bla ties at party meetings—for life.

A newspaper commented: "S came from below—like the s and like the people. She is t immortal star of the new Arge tina."

Workmen were told to st work for two days and observe days mourning.

All postage stamps are to withdrawn and a new memori issue put out at once.

No light radio programmes w be broadcast for 30 days and theatres are shut until after t funeral on Tuesday.

No horse-races will be run, eve sports stadium is shut, no r taurant or café may open.

And every man and woman the town of Santiago de Leste stayed up all last night as a sy bolic wake.

Demand for Eva Peron's remains

Buenos Aires, May 31.—Kidnappers of Lieutenant-General Pedro Aramburu, former Argentine president, today demanded the remains of Eva Perón in exchange for their prisoner. It was General Aramburu who ousted Eva Perón's husband from the presidency in 1955. The remains of a worker, Felipe Vallese, were also demanded.—Agence France Presse

Body of Eva Perón taken back to Argentina

From Our Correspondent
Buenos Aires, Nov 17

The embalmed body of Evita Perón, venerated as the "Little Madonna" by thousands of Argentina's poor, was brought back to Buenos Aires from Madrid early today.

President Isabel Perón, General Perón's third wife and political heir, accompanied by two sisters of Evita, headed a large committee of government and military officials as the remains were taken by car from the airport to the presidential chapel in Olivos, on the outskirts of Buenos Aires. Thousands of people lined the route, throwing flowers at the car.

Señora Perón, in a radio and television address to the nation last night, announced the return of Evita's body, calling her "the spiritual leader of the nation".

She said the "sacred" remains of Evita would lie, together with those of General Perón at the Olivos Chapel, from where they would be eventually transferred to the Altar of the Fatherland, the mausoleum at present being built in a Buenos Aires suburb.

Maria Evita Duarte de Perón was one of the most impressive and forceful political figures Argentina has produced. A former actress, in 1945 she became General Perón's second wife and helped her husband's political career by organizing mass political rallies among the working class and her *descamisados*—"shirtless ones". With their votes Perón won a crashing victory at the polls.

Beautiful and elegant, Evita spent millions of pounds of public money on the poor and her *descamisados* before dying of cancer in 1952 at the age of 33.

Her death created a religious fervour throughout the country and people petitioned the Vatican to have her canonized.

After the military overthrow of General Perón in 1955 Evita's body was taken from her shrine at the Confederation of Labour's headquarters in Buenos Aires.

Up till 1971, the whereabouts of the body remained a mystery, when at the instigation of the military government of General Lanusse her remains were returned secretly to General Perón, who was at the time living in Madrid.

For almost 16 years, Evita had lain in a secret grave under the name of a nun in a Milan cemetery.

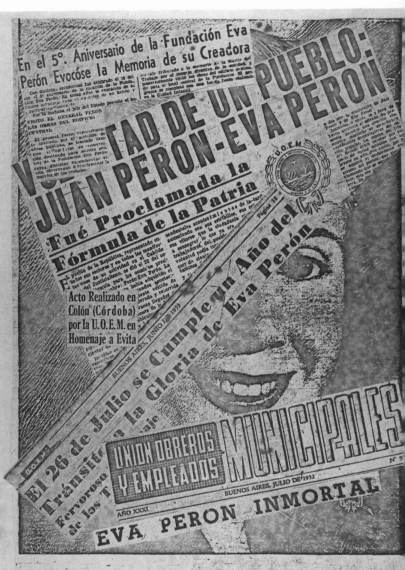

JEFA ESPIRITUAL DE LA NACION

PROSIGUIO EL DESFILE ANTE EL FERETRO DE EVA PERON

A LO LARGO DE UN EXTENSO RECORRIDO FORMARON DE NUEVO DENSAS COLUMNAS

Delegaciones gremiales del Gran Buenos Aires y del interior del país llegaron para rendir homenaje a la memoria de la esposa del jefe del Estado

Se declararán delegados gremiales en el Congreso

ORGANIZANSE LOS ACTOS DE MAÑANA Y EL DOMINGO

La policía adoptó medidas para ordenar la circulación del público

SE HAN FIJADO LIMITACIONES AL PARO GENERAL

Ha impartido instrucciones la Confederación General del Trabajo

UNA PROCESION DE ANTORCHAS SE HARA EN CORDOBA

Por tres días suspendiéronse las actividades en la Universidad

CORDOBA, 7 — Hanse acordado...

Funeral del Ministerio de Industria y Comercio

Asociación Gremial del Docente de la Facultad de Odontología

Fondo del Partido Peronista Femenino

De la Marina Mercante

Corporación del Caldén

Sindicato Obrero de Conservación Sanitaria y Afines

Federación Argentina de Voley-Ball

Asociación Cultural y Deportiva Adelante

LA CONFERENCIA DEL PACIFICO SE CLAUSURO AYER

Australia, N. Zelandia y los E. Unidos reafirmaron su colaboración

HONOLULU, 7 (AP)—Las reuniones de Australia, Nueva Zelandia y los Estados Unidos terminaron...

El Pacto y las actividades terroristas

El estacionamiento de vehículos

El DEFICIT EN LA ECONOMIA FRANCESA

LA EXPORTACION DE LANA DEL URUGUAY

MONTEVIDEO, 7 (De)...

MODIFICARAN EL PLAN DE REARME

WASHINGTON, 7 (AP)—Se espera que los miembros del comité de servicios armados...

NO SE REANUDO LA CONFERENCIA SOBRE EL SARRE

PARIS, 7 (The New York Times)...

EN COREA HUBO PROTESTAS DE LOS COMUNISTAS

MUYSAN, 7 (AP)—Los comunistas...

Desagrada en Londres la actitud de los dominios

LONDRES, 7 (AFP)...

SABESE QUIENES VAN A DIRIGIR EL PLAN SCHUMAN

Se publicó en París la lista de personas que formarán la Autoridad

PARIS, 7 (De)...

La acción en tierra

Comisión económica

Actividad aérea

LOS PRODUCTOS EN LOS MERCADOS EXTERIORES

EL TIEMPO